Praise for *It's Never Too Late to Be Your Self*

"The challenge of discovering our deeper identity—our most authentic self, which is the wellspring of our heart's desires—is the topic my dear friend Dr. Davina Kotulski addresses so ably in *It's Never Too Late to Be Your Self.* Drawing on her own experience of awakening to her desire for a more authentic expression of her essence and drawing from the lives of her clients and others to illustrate what this requires in practical terms, she shows us how we can step courageously out of a mindset that limits us and enter into the joy of living from our hearts. As you read, you'll learn how to reach for your potential even in the face of paralyzing fear."
—**Shefali Tsabary, Ph.D.,** New York Times bestselling author of *The Conscious Parent* and *The Awakened Family*

"It's Never Too Late to Be Your Self is a tender, wise guide for discovering, activating, and expressing the innate capacities of the human heart. Through her rich experience as a therapist and her own personal journey, Dr. Davina invites us to relate to ourselves and our world with a heart of compassion and courage. By weaving together insights of psychology and spirituality, she shows us how to skillfully do so."
—**Michael Bernard Beckwith,** bestselling author of *Spiritual Liberation* and *Life Visioning*

"It's Never Too Late to Be Your Self boldly invites us to step out in faith and self-love to be who we came here to be. It shows how to set aside our masks and let go of all fear and victimhood. Gently guiding us out of the limitations of our head and into the wisdom of our heart, where anything is possible, it teaches us how to follow our dreams. We discover what it means to love ourselves and others more than we ever thought possible and the importance of practicing forgiveness—something I couldn't be more passionate about on the journey to self-recognition and self-realization. If you are at all fainthearted, *It's Never Too Late to Be Your Self* will show you how to build your heart muscle so that you can move through fear into fulfillment. I love this book and know you will too."
—**Colin C. Tipping,** international bestselling author of *Radical Forgiveness* and *Radical Self-Forgiveness*

"A perfect, must-read book for anyone following a creative path. Be it the arts, business, or simply in the pursuit of an authentic life, *It's Never Too Late to Be Your Self* will help you move through obstacles, so you can stay true to your dreams. As a life coach, Davina's inspirational guidance has helped me to achieve quantifiable results on the path to fulfilling my creative dreams. This book captures the wisdom, humor, and thoughtfulness that Davina brings to each one of my sessions with her. Leading people to self-discovery and personal growth is her gift and this book is a natural extension of that talent."
—**Paul Bartholomew,** actor and announcer for *The Ellen Show*

"Let Davina's open-hearted enthusiasm guide you step by step to living from your courageous heart. Her book takes you by the hand and shows you what is possible, in your work, relationships, and beyond, when you follow the guidance of your heart."
—HeatherAsh Amara, author of *Warrior Goddess Training* and *Awakening Your Inner Fire*

"I've experienced my own version of coming to the edge and following my heart. I know there are so many people standing at that edge that could benefit from Davina's insightful guide. Thank you for shining light on the path of being the Truth of ourselves and doing what is ours to do."
—**Kathy Hearn**, Dean, Centers for Spiritual Living School of Spiritual Leadership

"In her new book *It's Never Too Late to Be Your Self,* Dr. Davina Kotulski shares how to have a courageous heart drawing from her own life experiences and those whom she has deeply inspired through her leadership, profound presence, and guidance to defy gravity and live from the truth of their hearts. Her own courageous heart and compassionate strength is woven throughout this book. *It's Never Too Late to Be Your Self* is a deep, yet fun, read."
—**Becky Robbins**, artist, humanitarian, and former vice-president of Robbins Research International

"In order to take your life forward, you have to take it back—from the downward-pulling forces that rob you of vitality. Davina Kotulski has written a simple, straight-

shooting, user-friendly guide to doing just that. With tremendous wisdom and compassion, and a visceral understanding of the hard, human work involved in opening—and trusting—the heart, she will help you navigate the rubber-meets-the-road work of putting more life in your life."
—**Gregg Levoy**, author of *Callings* and *Vital Signs*

"In this powerful, life-changing book, Dr. Davina Kotulski guides us to the inner recesses of our hearts where we discover the authentic Self. Through powerful stories and her own personal experience, Davina skillfully and compassionately walks us through this inner journey showing how to release fear and step into the freedom that is our divine birthright."
—**Joan Steadman, D.D.**, Agape Bay Area: A Center for Awakened Living

"Davina was a cutting-edge leader in the marriage equality movement and continues to be a passionate spiritual advocate. In her most recent book, *It's Never Too Late to Be Your Self*, she combines her experience and wisdom as a psychologist, life coach, and new thought spiritual practitioner to teach you how to create powerful positive change on the personal level. A great book for anyone who desires to live a fulfilling life beyond fear as Davina encourages the reader to do in this engaging book."
—**Mark Anthony Lord**, author of *Thou Shalt Not Suffer* and founder, Bodhi Spiritual Center

"We live in a time where truth and authenticity are being demanded of us. We can either follow the expectations of our cultural systems and conform and live an unfulfilled life or we can step into our divine power and claim our happiness; maybe even joy. Dr. Davina's book *It's Never Too Late to Be Your Self* is an inspirational and handy guide to reclaiming your true and powerful self and listening to the loving guidance of your heart."

—**Peter Bedard,** author of *Convergence Healing*

"Davina Kotulski reveals her own authentic heart in *It's Never Too Late to Be Your Self*. She has fearlessly stepped above the typical well-worn path in search for self, clarity, and happiness. Davina is a master weaver of compelling stories derived from the poignant crossroads between her clients and herself. She consistently demonstrates how digging deep into her own heart led her to the development of easy-to-follow pathways toward living a more genuine and joyful life. Read this whenever you are facing a crossroad to help lead you to your correct turn."

—**Renee Baribeau,** wind whistler, soul coach, and author of *Winds of Spirit*

"Davina skillfully delivers on her promise of building the reader's heart muscle. She draws a clear road map on how to communicate effectively with our hearts, unleashing our courage so that we may reach our highest potential and live the lives we envision for ourselves. This book will definitely inspire you to claim your own power."
—**Roma Khetarpal**, author of *The "Perfect" Parent* and founder, Tools of Growth

"*It's Never Too Late to Be Your Self* is a fantastic guide on how to connect with your deep 'inner knowing.' It's packed with practical and poignant lessons on how to shed anxiety and to live with more ease and flow—all the time. If you feel like life is weighing you down, read this book, use Davina's wisdom, and start living large again!"
—**Mark D. Langford**, CEO, C-Synergy, and author of *Thank God It's Wednesday*

IT'S NEVER TOO LATE TO BE YOUR SELF

FOLLOW YOUR INNER COMPASS AND TAKE BACK YOUR LIFE

Davina Kotulski, Ph.D.

LOS ANGELES, CALIFORNIA

Grateful acknowledgment is made for permission to reprint an excerpt from "Little Gidding" from *Four Quartets* by T.S. Eliot. Copyright © 1942 by T.S. Eliot, renewed 1970 by Esme Valerie Eliot. Reprinted by permission of Houghton Mifflin Harcourt Publishing Company.

Names and identifying details of the author's clients have been changed to protect client confidentiality. Any actual names included are those of individuals in the public domain or people who have agreed to be identified. Although every effort was made to ensure that the information in this book was correct at press time, the author and publishers do not assume, and hereby disclaim, any liability to any party for any loss, damage, or disruption caused by errors or omissions, whether such errors or omissions result from negligence, accident, or any other cause.

Red Ink Press/Davina Kotulski
1000 Fremont Ave #206 South Pasadena, CA. 91030
RedInkPressBooks.com

Copy Editing by Stephanie Gunning
Cover Design by Gus Yoo
Book Layout ©2019 Book Design Templates

Ordering Information:
Quantity sales. Special discounts are available on quantity purchases by corporations, associations, and others. For details, contact the publisher at the address or website above.

Library of Congress Control Number: 2018957919

ISBN 978-0-9978379-2-6 (paperback)

To my parents,
Janice Duchon and Richard Kotulski

Contents

Foreword

SHEFALI TSABARY, PH.D.

This is a book about being true to yourself, and I can't think of a more important topic. Yet so few of us are actually true to ourselves. It's for this reason that we are plagued with anxiety, aren't happy to the degree we'd like to be, and fail to find the deep fulfillment and sense of meaning for which we long.

We grow up in families, an educational system, and a society that teach us to please our "betters" at any cost, rather than be true to ourselves. The result is that we end up leading lives that are in many ways a betrayal of who we really are.

As author of three books on parenting, including the Oprah-acclaimed *The Conscious Parent,* a focus on helping children grow up to be true to themselves is my specialty. We can only ever be truly successful at any endeavor—in our personal life, as a parent, in a relationship, or in a career—to the degree that we truly know ourselves.

The challenge of discovering our deeper identity—our most authentic self, which is the wellspring of our heart's desires—is the topic my dear friend Dr. Davina Kotulski addresses so ably in *It's Never Too Late to be Your Self: Follow Your Inner Compass and Take Back Your Life.* Drawing on her own experience of awakening to her desire for a more authentic expression of her essence, and illustrating from the lives of her clients and others what this requires in practical terms, she shows us how we can step courageously out of a mindset that limits us and enter into the joy of living from our heart. As you read, you'll learn how to reach for your potential even in the face of paralyzing fear.

Davina has solid ground beneath her when she speaks of how we can transform our lives. She worked for years as a psychotherapist in the federal prison system in California, learning how to address human beings in their most dire states. She followed this up with a rich career in counseling individuals and families in her own private practice in the San Francisco Bay Area and now in the Los Angeles area, during which time she also developed her writing ability, becoming a published author. Her description of the places, people, and events that played a role in transforming her own life and the lives of others make this present book a particular delight to read.

In addition to her wealth of experience in the counseling profession, Davina shines in her personal life as well. She has had the courage to be at the forefront of a national movement for equality, pursuing her own heart's convictions even when these flew in the face of the expectations of others.

It's Never Too Late to Be Your Self isn't a prescription for fulfillment, whereby the author tells you what to do, as is so often the case with self-help books. Rather, it places the emphasis on helping you to find your own way. Davina plumbs the depths of what connecting with your heart really requires.

It's Never Too Late to be Your Self is an invitation to enter into your own essential being, where you will discover for yourself the choices available to you, the potential that resides within you, and the courage to fly in the face of your fears.

Introduction

MICHAEL BERNARD BECKWITH
FOUNDER, AGAPE INTERNATIONAL
SPIRITUAL CENTER

Whether we say it out loud or mentally coach ourselves to have courage, we are activating a one-word mantra that causes us to instinctively pull our shoulders back, hold our heads high, and embolden our hearts. And with good reason, especially considering how etymology takes us back to the Old French of the thirteenth century when *corage* translated as "heart."

The book you hold in your hands is a wise, trustworthy guide into the shape-shifting terrain of heart-centered courage. Now to clarify, courage is not the absence of fear or a denial of the octopus grip fear can have on our psyche when we find ourselves standing on inner or outer shaky ground. And while courage also includes selfless, heroic acts under extraordinary circumstances that earn our awe and respect, Dr. Davina Kotulski focuses on the aspect of courage that is intrinsic to each of us and is applicable in our everyday lives. She defines courage as a quality that empowers us to get to know ourselves through and through, without judging what we observe, and embracing the entirety of our being. It is about finally giving ourselves permission to unconditionally open our hearts to ourselves, to our life purpose, and the path for aligning our intuitive guidance with that purpose. A heart set on courage does not always offer us convenient or comfortable guidance. What it does do is enable us to courageously befriend our fear and thereby escort ourselves beyond the inner boundaries we have established to maintain our sense of safety, security, and keep our ego and defense mechanisms intact. In other words, we begin authentically walking the hero's journey.

The truth is that in spite of life circumstances that can initiate fearful responses, our greatest fear can be of ourselves. *It's Never Too Late to Be Your Self* offers time-tested methods used by Davina in her sessions with private clients and through her public work with individuals across all spectrums of society for moving beyond that fear. The valuable tools she offers cause a vibrational shift within those who commit to practicing them as they discover and activate their innate courage while trusting that we live in a friendly, supportive universe. She teaches us how to make friends with ourselves and our circumstances so that we don't stifle our vulnerability and instead energize loving kindness toward ourselves, others, and our world.

Through her depth of experience as a therapist and spiritual practitioner, Davina shines a radiant light of practical wisdom and tenderness on the courage vibrating at the core of your being and yearning to express through you. So, sit back, breathe, and remember that it's never too late to be your self.

Part One

Tune In to Your Inner Compass

CHAPTER ONE

It's Never Too Late to Be Your Self

"The privilege of a lifetime is being who you are."
—Joseph Campbell

I took her arm as we climbed the steps of the Rialto Bridge. She was still getting used to her high heels. It was a beautiful spring evening in Venice, Italy. The warm night air was peppered with a crisp ocean breeze that drifted inland from the Adriatic. The lights from the *ristorantes* danced on the canals. We sat at a table alongside the Grand Canal, watching the gondoliers beckon tourists to glide across the mirrored water in their shiny black gondolas. She was dressed fashionably in a white blouse, black skirt, tights, and a shimmering pink Venetian scarf.

It was the first time in her life that Patricia had appeared openly as a woman.

It was also the first time she'd packed only women's clothing for a trip. Having come to Italy to attend my Seduce Your Muse workshop, Patricia was publicly claiming and proclaiming that she was a woman ready to set herself free from the man's body she had spent four decades hiding in. Through our work together, she had found the courage to free herself from society's norms and her false identity as Patrick.

We met at a networking event for people who owned their own businesses. Solopreneurs, we called ourselves. Patrick was a highly successful CEO of a medical company, able to hold his own with the good old boys, yet his heart yearned for something more. He wanted to create his own business—except that each time he tried, he felt blocked.

After I shared my story on the stage, Patrick approached me and asked to speak with me privately. As a result of this conversation, "he" hired me so that *she* could finally stop hiding.

One year later, we were having dinner on the Grand Canal, Patricia courageously living her truth, and me courageously living one of my dreams to bring people to one of the most beautiful cities on earth to help them tap into their creative wisdom and share their message with the world. It was as if we were here by divine appointment, both of us letting our hearts courageously lead our lives.

There are many ways to live authentically, though they may not be as dramatic as revealing your true gender identity or putting on international writing and healing retreats. Still, in my experience most of us have an aspect of our life in which we are hiding, holding back, playing small, squelching our dreams, denying our heart's desires, or in some way settling for less.

In a world where one out of twelve Americans is abusing substances,[1] one in eight is taking antidepressants, more than half feel disconnected from their jobs,[2] and greater numbers are reporting that they are unhappy in their relationships, it is important to find the courage to connect with your authentic essence, so you can start living a life you love.

People give many reasons for not being true to themselves. Fear of rejection, a tendency to try to please people, a hesitancy to take up too much space, a dread of making others uncomfortable, not trusting ourselves to know the right moves to make, a fear that life might not support us if we step out, or giving reality too much credit. Remember, reality is subjective, determined by our experiences and shaped by our thoughts and beliefs.

What has kept you from following your heart and moving in the direction of your dreams? What has kept you from your happiness? Is it a fear of looking selfish? Do you believe you won't get what you're going after? Do you feel that nothing you do matters?

In the end, all of these reasons come down to deciding whether or not we will choose what seems *practical* and *reasonable* rather than what truly *inspires us* and *brings us joy*.

Anti-Bliss

Many of us have an objection to feeling joyous. Something in us resists feeling wonderful, resists the fullness of life. We feel there's something flawed about us, something not quite right about who we are. Religious doctrine has contributed to this. For some people, this feeling is familiar and therefore comfortable.

Sebastian Moore, a gay English monk, referred to this state as *anti-bliss*. Anti-bliss is an inherent pessimism that he calls a "preference for the sad."[3] It is a state of struggle against the natural and spontaneous parts of ourselves that seek to become fully alive. It takes the shape of a huge resistance to the enjoyment of life. We want to be happy, but only so much. The fires of anti-bliss can be flamed from religious doctrine, as was the case for Moore. He saw how the teachings of original sin from the Catholic Church, and of course, the Church's position on same-sex love, kept him from connecting with his bliss and accepting himself.

Growing up in homes with domestic violence, mental illness, or alcoholism, or living in violent or war-torn regions can also contribute to the state of anti-bliss. In these environments individuals are conditioned to keep their heads down, to keep the volume turned down on their natural state of exuberance. Anti-bliss is like the force that pushes down the beach ball in the pool, keeping it from skimming along the top of the water and going along happily with the flow of life.

Bliss, as Joseph Campbell recognized, is our natural state. Yet, as Marianne Williamson shared eloquently in her book *A Return to Love,* which I will paraphrase here, we have a fear of being who we really are in all our magnificence. Something in us fights the bliss. Bliss arises spontaneously when our thoughts and reactions don't get in the way. Thoughts and reactions can block the feelings of our true self. You can see this bliss in a baby or very young children. It's there whenever nothing is disturbing them.

Anti-bliss isn't only a resistance to our own enjoyment of life, but antipathy to anyone else enjoying life in a way we deem immoral. It's what drives people to impose their standards on others—and with the force of law if they can swing it.

We also strangely believe that there's just so much happiness to go around, as if happiness were distributed like pieces of pie. We tell ourselves we are only entitled to a limited amount, less we take more than our fair share or rob someone else of their happiness quotient. We also believe that our happiness will hurt other people, which causes us to dim our radiance and live with far less joy than is possible. This is the phenomenon of anti-bliss.

Happiness is not a pie, though it may bring us a moment of pleasure going down. Happiness is not divided into a limited number of pieces. Happiness is the fundamental state of our being, the nature of our humanity. There's an infinite supply of happiness. We no longer need to be driven by the voice in the head, with its stories of fear, anger, grief, and guilt. We can choose to live in a state of bliss that entails listening to and following the heart, rather than anti-bliss and being driven by the mind.

Do you feel like you aren't living the life you want to live? Are you letting fear stop you from following your heart? Have you made changes, only to become discouraged by seeming setbacks? Do you find it hard to listen to and follow your own voice because the voices of society, your friends, and your family blare in your head? Are you concerned that if you choose happiness it will hurt others? Do you find yourself wanting to please others at the expense of pleasing yourself?

If you answered yes to any of these questions, you're not alone.

Many people who come to me for coaching or therapy also have these challenges. They want to live a more authentic life but feel paralyzed by outside forces dictating their choices. They find themselves shackled to unsatisfying jobs, stuck in relationships that don't excite them, and generally feeling unfulfilled.

I too know what it's like to be paralyzed by fear—and also what it's like to take back your life. For over twenty years, I've worked as a psychologist helping people uncover their essential selves. This book will share with you what I've learned about how to create a life that honors your authentic self-expression, which is the only path to ever feeling fulfilled.

You'll discover how to:

- Reconnect with your true essence and what really matters.
- Listen to your inner wisdom.
- Move forward in the face of fear and other obstacles.
- Commit to your dreams and take back your life.

Follow Your Heart

When you follow the teachings in this book, you will reclaim your life, and begin genuinely living from your true essence and heart's desires. For instance, my client Judy wanted to quit her successful day job and start her own company, but she was afraid of taking the risk—until she finally did it. Then there's Carl, whose fear of crossing bridges kept him from living in the city of his dreams until he conquered it. I also think of Maria, who, after twenty-five years in prison, was plagued by agoraphobia. Terrified by the idea of even going to the grocery store, through our work together Maria was finally able to face her fears and free herself. Oh, and there's Gloria, who had lived in the closet for her entire adult life and wanted to finally come out as a lesbian to her conservative Mexican family at age sixty. Well, she did!

Being yourself is about creating a life that brings out your talent, gifts, values, personal truths, sensibilities, and passions. It's about discovering what's in your heart, then having the courage to actualize your desires by stepping out with faith in yourself. For Mariana, it was moving from Florida to Los Angeles so she could realize her dream of being a celebrity fitness trainer. For Laura, it was becoming an intuitive spiritual counselor, which meant she first had to say yes to her psychic abilities and let go of her stalled marriage and Catholic guilt. For Claudette, it was releasing her inhibitions and starting to write erotic poetry that even made nonsmokers catch fire. For Eric, it was investing his money and energy to create an app despite his family's fear that he was squandering his time and treasure in an uncertain future. For Heidi, it was leaving her small town in Austria to pursue her desire to be a Broadway actress.

Begin Again

Being your authentic self isn't always about proactively choosing change. Sometimes it's about how you pick up the pieces and move forward with life when you suddenly find yourself in a major life transition through the loss of a marriage, a job, a home, or an important role in your life. As was the case with my client Maggie, who reconnected with her true essence and love of horses after her marriage of thirty-five years ended. She took her divorce settlement and moved to the country where she could afford to lease a horse. This was also true for my client Rebecca, who had put her dreams on hold to raise her children. After launching her last child, Rebecca picked up her guitar to become the singer/songwriter she was meant to be. And even for my client Johnny, who after suddenly being laid off by the corporation he worked for, invested his severance money in traveling. Traveling was something he'd always dreamed of doing, but had decided it was capricious. He'd learned this sentiment from his father, who had emphasized that success was measured by ten-hour days and big bonuses. When Johnny returned from his travels, he was clear about what really mattered to him and resolved to never trade happiness for money.

Each of these individuals represents hundreds of clients who have followed my approach and taken courageous action to live lives that honor their authentic core. Rather than being ruled by their fears, they now live in a way that expresses their bona fide choices. Beyond mere surviving, each of them is thriving.

This book will teach you how to reclaim your essence and authentic self-expression and live a life you love. This is not a self-help book, it is a *coming-into-your-power* book! With every story you read, along with following my step-by-step approach to courageous change, you'll grow in confidence and build a heart muscle that will allow you to live a life that honors your unique path.

What I'm going to share with you goes deeper than simply making radical changes on the outside. This book is about shifting the inner terrain, supporting you in becoming deeply connected to your essential nature, which will allow you to make choices from your true essence, not just rearranging the deck chairs on the Titanic.

The choice is yours to make. The chapters ahead are an invitation to follow a process I've created called hearticulation™, which will help you connect with your inner compass (your heart) and create a radically authentic life that you love. The journey is about being true to *you*. It's never too late to connect with your authentic center, your natural state of bliss, and begin again. The first step is opening your heart.

CHAPTER TWO

Open Your Heart

"When you live with an open heart, unexpected,
joyful things happen."
—*Oprah Winfrey*

The first organ we develop is the heart. We call it an organ, but it's actually the strongest muscle in the human body. The heart lies at the center of our four limbs. Its arteries and veins supply blood to the extremities of the body, with the average red blood cell circulating through the entire system about once each minute.

Eastern philosophical traditions identify seven energy centers, known as chakras, in the body. The heart, which is the fourth chakra, is considered the spiritual center of the body, acting as the fulcrum that connects the lower three earth-based chakras with the higher three celestial chakras. For mystics, both eastern and western, the heart is where heaven and earth meet.

It's no accident that we refer to the most important aspect of something as the *heart of the matter.*

Native American traditions speak of the importance of our connection to the heartbeat of Mother Earth, represented by the drum. When Native American drummers sit in a circle and drum out a unified beat, it represents not only the sacred heartbeat of creation but also the fact we are all connected, all ultimately one. Hence, the Lakota expression *Mitakuye oyasin* ("We are all are related") points to the interconnectedness of the entire creation.

On a quantum physics level, scientists are beginning to study and find truth in what indigenous cultures have long known and believed, that we are connected to a unified field of energy. According to its website, the HeartMath Institute has conducted experiments to "demonstrate how people are connected with one another through their own individual magnetic fields, which are generated primarily by the brain and, although much more so, the heart."[1] They call this research the *field view of reality.*

The HeartMath Institute has found that we have the power to use our personal fields of influence to uplift others.[2] One study showed how a boy in a different room was able to shift his dog's heart rate simply by connecting with his feelings of love for the dog and sending him loving thoughts. Another study showed that individuals utilizing a heart-based coherence technique could influence someone else's heart rhythm.[3] These studies show that positive intentions matched with a grateful heart create harmony.

And it's not just people in our immediate vicinity who benefit from our positive energy, we can also impact people far away. The HeartMath Institute reports: "human bioemotional energy can have a subtle, but significant (scientifically measurable) nonlocal effect on people, events, and organic matter."[4]

Therefore, if we extrapolate from the early findings of their research, it is quite possible that when we are connected to our essence and living authentically, our happiness, which creates coherence in the shared energy field, plays a part in uplifting the planet. This research suggests that following our bliss makes the world a better place. How cool is that?

Imagine it. When you are true to your self, you are contributing to the health and happiness of the planet and all of its inhabitants great and small.

However, what if, when you are suffering, hiding your light, engaged in drudgery and trying to make it through another day, frustrated and unfulfilled, you are contributing to the field of negativity in our emotional stratosphere? On days you're bummed out, you're contributing to the global sense of unease and disquiet on the planet. Whenever it sucks to be you, it sucks for everyone else too.

Now let me be clear, the kind of happiness I'm referring to is not about glitz and glitter. I'm not talking about feeding your "hungry ghost," the Buddhist term for consumerism and trying to fill the empty spots inside of you with distraction and endless pleasure. I'm talking about the authentic joy and contentment that come from living life from your inner essence. Authenticity often includes things like being open and honest about your sexual orientation, if you haven't been, or following your authentic calling rather than simply punching a time clock. However, being your true self goes even deeper than this and requires the courage to open your heart. Being openhearted will transform the quality of your life. As such, opening your heart is a worthy end in itself. Opening your heart can also serve as a means of becoming more deeply connected with your heart's desires, which define your calling.

Time to Take Heart

The word *courage* comes from the Latin *cor,* meaning "heart." Courage is having the confidence to act in line with our convictions and passions, which are a heart-related matter. It involves our ability to face difficulty, danger, and pain with bravery. The expression "to take heart" means to revive your courage.

To have courage is to have a strong heart, and to live from your heart requires an act of courage. Opening your heart is the basis for living a life aligned with your true essence. When I speak of *living from your heart* what I mean is being guided by the more fluid and open parts of yourself, connecting with joy, being open to life, being led by intuition, emotion, and feeling, and following hunches. What I mean by *living from the head* involves basing your decisions solely on logic, analysis, and reason.

Many of us resist opening our hearts, let alone following them, which keeps us from connecting with our deepest desires. One of the key reasons for our resistance is the cynicism toward matters of the heart we've grown up with. For those raised by authoritarian parents or in a country where expressing feelings is considered a weakness, following your heart may be seen as foolish, reckless, and even potentially harmful. Despite what we might see depicted in romantic Hollywood movies, western culture values intellectual intelligence over emotional intelligence, left brain over right brain. For instance, we're warned, "Don't wear your heart on your sleeve." It's no wonder that so many of us experience strong resistance to listening to the wisdom of our hearts.

You may also find yourself resisting opening your heart and letting it guide you because at some point in the past you followed your heart and got burned. When we get hurt, we tell ourselves it's stupid to listen to our hearts and much safer and wiser to listen to our heads. If you've been blocking out a lot of pain, and you start opening your heart again, you may find yourself feeling sad, confused, or disappointed in yourself and others. You may also feel just plain scared. These all are natural reactions to opening your heart after you've been hurt.

However, if you don't close your heart, but instead allow it to continue opening, you'll find that you spontaneously begin to move *through* the pain toward a *natural joyfulness* that's long been hidden deep within you. As you become aware of the contrast between the hurt feelings you've carried and the joy that's beginning to well up from within you, you'll see that, in each moment, life presents you with a choice. You can opt to stay in your pain, or you can decide to go with that emerging contentedness. When you embrace your wellbeing and turn your back on past hurts, a whole new life opens up before you.

As your heart opens, you will begin to feel deep inner peace, like the way you feel when you take a walk, go for a drive in the country, sit down on a bench, or visit a flower garden. You're doing something that feels good. You are in love with life, and you find yourself flowing into the action. You experience no resistance because your heart is called in the direction you're flowing.

When you are in your heart, you feel good in your body. Your breathing is deep and peaceful. Life feels full and enjoyable. You feel expansive and trust that life is working out for you. You also feel grateful for the people in your life, blessed to share this life experience with them. They matter to you, and therefore you are generous with your time, talents, and affection. It's easy to give, and it's easy to receive. There's a reciprocity, and you feel no fear of being taken advantage of because all of your interactions with others come from your heart. Heart-centered being is so different from the cutthroat mentality of survival that mars so many of our relationships as human beings.

This same feeling of being comfortable in your world spills over into the world of nature around you. Instead of being in a rush, you don't mind taking that extra minute to stop and smell a flower, or even to jump out of your car and take a picture of a stunning sunset, a beautiful landscape, or something whimsical. You are now beginning to feel at home with yourself, and you are open to experience the flow of life and to connect with your self on a deeper level.

My Heart Be Still

Just as a physician needs the room to be quiet when she takes out her stethoscope to listen to a patient's heartbeat, slowing down and becoming quiet is the key to listening to your heart. To listen to our hearts, we must be present in what we are doing. With this in mind, you can see why multitasking, being distracted by the television in the background, looking at email when you need to be focused on something, or otherwise getting caught up in the rush of life can keep you from connecting with your true essence.

A characteristic of our essence is that we experience it as a quiet, felt knowing. I would describe this inner knowing as an absolute stillness. It involves no concepts, beliefs, or values.

Quite the opposite of urging us in one direction or another, like the ever-present voices in our head do, this stillness is characterized by a feeling of total calm.

Stillness quiets the ego and awakens the soul, the source of deeper wisdom within you.

When we experience this stillness in ourselves, a quiet knowing arises. Some might call this a *divine download*. This simple and uncomplicated knowing is unlike any other state we ever experience. We just know whatever we need to know without having to conceptualize it. This is the simple clarity I experienced when I knew I had to quit my government job.

Let me be clear: This voice speaks to us only in the present moment, not in the form of past regret or as a future projection. When we feel guilty about something we've done, that's an emotional reaction. When we run a future scenario in our head and become attached to an outcome, we hear our thoughts and the emotions they trigger, not our inner being. When we hear a cast of critics chastising our actions we are in the territory of the mind, not the heart.

Additionally, your mind will try to get you to either take action or avoid action to keep you from experiencing fear. So, it's important to recognize that when it's your head that's running the show, its efforts will be devoted to moving you away from fear, protecting you, and pushing you to avoid any situation that elicits a sense of wanting. Your head will leave you with a vague sense that something bad will happen if you pursue a particular course of action or a feeling that something will be taken from you.

This is the opposite of a sense of peace and the feeling you are doing something in line with your heart's desires.

Seeking comfort, the mind will steer you away from something you fear, *an urging that has a fundamentally different feeling to it than the heart guiding you toward something you love.* The call of the heart is *always* toward a fuller expression of your authentic self and a greater manifestation of the love that's your true nature.

Your head will try to keep you safe and escape discomfort by persuading you to stick with your old programming. Furthermore, it will attempt to talk you out of doing the very thing that's in alignment with your heart's desire and soul's calling.

When a situation arises in your life that triggers a tinge of self-doubt, you are now faced with a choice. To which voice do you listen? The one that arises from your essence and encourages you to plunge into the fullness of joy? Or the one that says, "You see, you have all these problems. You're confused. Who are you kidding? You don't know what you're doing. You're ruining everything. You screwed up. You're a mess. You're hopeless. You're never going to amount to anything!" That's the voice of anti-bliss attempting to trump our original bliss, which is our authentic state. Preserving your authentic state is why it's so essential for you to be able to discern when you're in your head and when you're in your heart.

Awakening to our true essence is why each of us must break with the norm, which is step two in the hearticulation process.

INVITATION

Today, notice the voice you are listening to in whatever situations arise in your life. Is it a confused voice in your head or the still knowing of your heart? Which voice will you follow? How are you discerning the difference? Where do you notice it in your body? Is your breathing deep or shallow? Is your breath rate slow and relaxed? Notice your facial muscles. Are they relaxed or tense? Where are your shoulders, are they relaxed or up to your ears? Is your body language open and expansive or tight and closed? Just begin to notice how it feels in your body when you are listening to your heart or your head. What are the differences?

CHAPTER THREE

Awaken to Your Authentic Self

"To thine own self be true, and it must follow, as the night the day, thou canst not then be false to any man."
—*William Shakespeare*

Tom Shadyac is a wildly successful Hollywood movie director and screenwriter. He was the youngest joke writer to work with Bob Hope and has several Golden Globes under his belt. With his fortune, he purchased a 17,000-square-foot mansion, multiple cars, and a plane. Not too shabby.

In 2007, Tom had a horrible bicycle accident and hit his head. It was a wake-up call. Tom says, "I was standing in the house that my culture had taught me was a measure of the good life. I was struck with one very clear, very strange feeling: I was no happier."

Following his accident, Tom began to see how our culture programs us with ideas of success that place a premium on materialism but don't serve our highest good. He realized that what he wanted most was a simple life. He sold his mansion, his plane, and his cars, then moved into a mobile home. You'd think he would have gotten rid of the bicycle, but it was one of the few things that moved with him.

Tom says he's happier now than when he had all the extravagances of his former life. "True success is intrinsic," he explains. "It's love. It's kindness. It's community. People find happiness in direct proportion to doing what they love."

He adds, "If you don't do what you love, you die a little every day."

Tom made a documentary about his life, entitled *I AM,* to encourage people to follow their hearts. He wanted them to ask themselves who they are and what they really want, as opposed to what their culture has told them they ought to be or ought to want.

Come Alive

The experience Tom Shadyac describes in his movie comes as a wake-up call to many of us. Suddenly we are aware that the "normal" state of things, what we might call the "good life," is leaving us dead inside.

As we grow up, our family and culture teach us to hide our true identity. So eventually, we're all going around pretending to be our real self, when in reality we're out of touch with our authentic essence.

The term *authentic* originates from the Latin *authenticus,* which means "coming from the author," as well as from the

Greek word *authentes*, "one who acts independently." The word is rooted in the notion that you could author your life by acting independently of others—meaning, act independently of what others want for you, what you believe you are capable of, or what society or family members tell you to do.

In modern usage, the most common meanings for the word *authentic* are something that's genuine, the real deal, as well as something that's accurate, trustworthy, reliable. In other words, authenticity carries the attributes of genuineness, in the sense of being your original self, along with trustworthiness. When you are living your authentic life, people will value your originality and trust you. They will see you as the real deal.

Since losing touch with ourselves is so commonplace, it doesn't occur to us that the things we've been taught to value and chase after, imagining they will bring us satisfaction, are divorced from our deepest being. Sometimes we experience a collision between who we think we are and our authentic self, as was Tom's case, but more frequently it happens in subtle ways.

The process of awakening to your authentic self may begin with a feeling that you are losing yourself—it could be in your work, an important relationship, or your overall lifestyle. A serious dissatisfaction with life as you've known it surfaces, shattering your pretenses. For Tom Shadyac, this happened in a sudden burst of insight. With many of my clients, it's a process.

What are you experiencing? Is the split between your true self and the identity you've created at odds? Are you experiencing anxiety? Are you disheartened or depressed?

The anxious state so many of us experience daily is the result of leading a divided life. This state may show up as a need to prove ourselves. We may adopt the image of a champion, struggling to make our mark in the world, driven by ego. Or we may feel hopeless, which may show up in self-destructive behavior, such as excessive drinking, not taking care of ourselves, self-mutilation, or even suicide.

Though the person who soars to the pinnacle of success may appear fundamentally different from the depressed addict, *both* are driven by anxiety, self-doubt, and a sense of inadequacy, and guilt. They are two sides of the same coin.

We all carry within us the sense that there is something fundamentally flawed with us. This belief creates a sense of shame over our very being, which leads us to believe we aren't good enough, deserving enough, and perhaps not even worthy to *be* here.

These feelings originate from having experienced the disapproval of who we are, and the subsequent suppression, or even repression, of ourselves, our true essence. The fact that we are unconscious of our true being generates the anxiety.

We intuitively sense that something about us isn't *real*.

The submerged parts of us want to resurface. Therefore, in ways we are unconscious of, the essential self—that which some call the *soul*—exerts its desire to come alive.

The soul's *modus operandi* is to subvert the comfortable existence we create for ourselves. It may do this in subtle surreptitious ways, or in a manner that shocks us back to life. Think of the song lyrics of Springsteen's *Hungry Heart* where he talks about going out for a drive in his car and then never returning to his wife and children. While the song may suggest we can simply abandon our responsibilities, it's not about abandoning our responsibilities. It's about remaining awake to life so we can make conscious choices. It's also about staying connected to our heart's desires and authentic self, so we don't abandon ourselves and as a result find ourselves so off course from our true nature in life that we are unconsciously propelled to reclaim our lives for ourselves in drastic ways that can be harmful to ourselves and others.

Conscious choices, not reactions, are the territory of the courageous heart. Honoring your authentic self means mindfully speaking your truth and then leaning into it, which is a far cry from running away or disappearing. It's about embodying your choices. Sometimes those conscious choices include ending agreements or commitments that no longer serve your highest good, or anyone else's for that matter.

It can be a shock when we leave a relationship, walk out of a job, or move to a different location, even another country, often without any real understanding of what we are doing, yet knowing we must do so if we are to have any integrity to our soul.

We can't let our false selves live our lives. The false self must die. Then the true self, the one we've kept hidden, can surface.

Death and Rebirth

Terces Englehart, the cofounder of Café Gratitude, once said that we create at our level of consciousness and as we continue to grow, we will reach points in our lives where what we've created at one level of consciousness no longer reflects who we have become. So, to continue growing and create something new, we must let go of the old. We must shed the old skin, rather than trying to continue to make it fit. Letting go is similar to letting the false self die.

Even though we know our false self must "die," the process is still painful. Death is never a pleasant occurrence. The experience of awakening to our real selves can be terrifying—and yet it's precisely by embracing this terror, this death of who we have imagined ourselves to be, that we move beyond fear and into fulfillment. It's when we feel we can't go on like this any longer—we just can't do it anymore—that we surrender to the death of the false self and life as we've known it. Surrender is when rebirth becomes possible.

When we feel ourselves imploding, as if our whole world is collapsing, this is the moment we give birth to the authentic self. To be a therapist in the presence of individuals making this transition is a privilege. I get to walk alongside them in their journeys, and at times midwife their rebirth.

For example, let's look to my client, Katie, from St. Louis, who relocated to San Jose with her boyfriend, Jake, after he'd gotten a great tech job. Katie was more than happy to get out of the Midwest and break suffocating ties with her family. She'd been with Jake since college, and he was the perfect boyfriend for that chapter of her life. They studied together and supported each other in moving toward their dreams.

After moving across the country with Jake, Katie realized that she was now free to dream bigger than her family's expectations for her to marry and settle down. She'd always wanted to pursue her dream as a writer. While she loved Jake, the two had little in common beyond their shared experiences of growing up. He was content playing video games with his friends online while she wanted to be a part of a bigger community.

Katie confided in me that she'd known that she and Jake ultimately were not compatible before the move, but she had tried to quell her misgivings about him because he was such a loving and supportive guy. Despite this, once in California, she felt the disparities between them even more. I worked with Katie to support her in sharing her truth with Jake. He was sad but understood and agreed. Katie felt relieved. However, she had a hard time letting Jake go. He'd been a close friend and confidant for so many years. He was her security blanket, and she went through several months of grieving as she moved to San Francisco to begin her new life.

A few months after the breakup, Jake began dating a coworker. Within a year he was engaged to this new woman.

Katie slowly began building a new circle of friends as she moved through her feelings of sadness. She was able to confront her parents about their ongoing comments that she'd made a huge mistake and was "never going to find as good a guy as Jake." She also challenged their expectations for her, ignoring their insistence that she return to the Midwest following the breakup. We also worked on her negative internal dialogue, which included such comments as "You will die an old maid," and "You will never find love again."

It was easy to see how much courage Katie had to muster to follow her heart. If she'd just gone along with the program, or the programming from her parents, she wouldn't have had to face her parents' disapproval or the emotional storm that ensued as she struck out on her own. On the other hand, something inside of her would be quietly dying.

When people stay in inauthentic situations, their unhappiness surfaces through overeating, daily drinking, porn addictions, shopping addictions, affairs, health issues, depression, anxiety, and so on. While leaving an unhappy situation may be painful, remaining in one is detrimental to our wellbeing in the long-term.

Katie may have had to deal with uncertainty, sadness, standing up for herself, setting boundaries, and taking risks, and while that was uncomfortable for her, at the end of the day she knew she was living her authentic life.

About six months after ending her relationship with Jake, Katie was regularly attending a weekly writing group and getting great feedback on her writing. She developed a crush on one of the other writers, and they began dating. Almost a year later, Katie got her first job as a writer for an established magazine. She enjoyed living in San Francisco and felt like her life was engaging and full of possibility. She was still dating the writer guy and happy to be in a relationship with a man who shared her enthusiasm for literature.

As was the case with Katie, when we loosen our ties with everything that up to this point has given us our reason for being, we experience a coming together of all those aspects of ourselves that we previously did not allow to coexist. Once we allow the ego, or the false self, to die, there's a reverence for our new life, a sacredness to everything we do.

Out of the darkness, the confusion, the anguish of this death of a false identity, there crystalizes a new sense of ourselves, a new purpose, a new meaning for everything we do—even when what we do after the death may not be all that different on the outside, who we are on the inside has been transformed.

We find ourselves spontaneously following our "bliss." Our center of gravity has shifted from head to heart, restoring the mind to its rightful place in service to the heart. Now we must begin to engage in practices that support us in staying connected to our deeper self, which is step three in the hearticulation process.

In the next chapter, you'll learn ways to anchor yourself to your authentic essence.

INVITATION

Take a look at your life. Is there anywhere you are being inauthentic? Where are you hiding or not expressing your true feelings or your true self? Where have you numbed out? What aspects of your life feel dead? What is happening in your life that you are tolerating or muscling through? Where are you just going through the motions? What is your ego holding on to that your heart wants to release? What are your real values? What would it be like to live a life that honored your values and heart's desires?

CHAPTER FOUR

Connect with Your Deeper Essence

"Life moves pretty fast. If you don't stop and look around once in a while, you could miss it."
—*Ferris Bueller*, Ferris Bueller's Day Off

Have you noticed that whenever you drive a familiar route, there are sometimes long periods when you are zoned out? Perhaps you don't remember passing some of the places you know you had to drive by to arrive at your destination. You ask yourself, *Did I pass the gas station yet? Did I miss my turn?* You were on autopilot.

Many of us are in an almost trancelike state in other important areas of our life. We're not even conscious of being in our bodies. We're going through the motions to get to the next thing rather than being present and connected to ourselves.

I find great wisdom in Thich Nhat Hanh's statement, "The Buddha said, 'The past no longer exists, and the future is not here yet.' There is only a single moment in which we can truly be alive, and that is the present moment. Being present in the here and now is our practice."[1]

Most of us live in our heads. We dwell on the past, such as wondering whether we said or did the right thing. We also spend time stressing about the future, worrying about the many "what if" scenarios we devise with our incessant thinking. We focus on regrets, expectations, to-do lists, the "not enough," and the "next time." Our shoulders are up to our ears. People around us irritate us. We feel rushed, hurried, and may find ourselves constantly riding someone's butt, changing lanes, and cursing under our breath.

Because our minds move quickly from thought to thought, we frequently miss the beauty and joy of the present. This sentiment is expressed in a joke one of my Native American friends shared in a healing group we were coleading. "If you've got one foot in the past, and one foot in the future, what are you doing? Answer: You're pissing all over the present." I think that aptly sums it up.

None of this anxious thinking about situations past, present, or future has anything to do with who we *really* are.

If you want to move beyond fear and live a fulfilling life, you have to release the mind's fears and regrets. You do this by anchoring yourself in the present moment and connect with your deeper self.

In the pages that follow, you will find key practices that I recommend to my clients which have helped them do just that.

Surround Yourself with Beauty

The *Diné* (Navajo) adhere to a way of life they call the *beauty way*. This term refers to the beauty that exists within us and outside us. According to the Diné, the beauty way is our true essence. When we live in alignment with the beauty way (our authentic nature), and we revere Mother Earth and her inhabitants, life unfolds harmoniously in divine order.

Have you ever noticed that when beauty surrounds you, it's easier to feel at peace? When we surround ourselves with beauty, it mirrors our beautiful inner space—our formless essence. It reminds us of who we have always been. The heart resonates with things that are beautiful. We can find beauty in nature, and we can create beauty in our homes and workplaces.

How Do We Create Beauty?

We can create beauty in our environments by bringing in simple objects to beautify the space. Buy yourself some flowers or a plant. Pick out some aromatic candles and attractive candleholders. Natural elements in your home or work are grounding and connect us to our essential nature.

Place stones, crystals, pinecones, and colorful fabrics in places that will add life to your environment. Invest in paintings, photos, or other art that feels good to you and decorate your home and office with things that you enjoy. Taking time to bring beauty into your living space will lift your spirits.

I'm sure you've heard the phrase cleanliness is next to godliness. This colloquialism resonates with me because when I enter a clean, well-cared for space, I feel more relaxed and connected to life. Cleaning our spaces, dusting them, taking out the trash, and such, allows us to be more fully present and vibrant in the space, rather than being distracted by old energy.

This principle applies to the objects that occupy the spaces you occupy. You want to be mindful of what you bring into your physical space. Take a look at what's already in your space. Are the objects in your home or office there intentionally? Do you feel good when you look at them? Do you keep things that you don't like because they were gifts?

In her book *The Life-Changing Magic of Tidying Up*, Marie Kondo emphasizes the importance of only keeping items that bring you joy. She says to "truly cherish things that are important to you, you must first discard those that have outlived their purpose."[2]

When you clear or release things that you no longer want or need, you will "feel clear and refreshed," so she advises that you "keep only things that speak to your heart."[3] Clearing clutter will bring back your vitality and help you connect more deeply with your true essence. After all, if you can't clear your room of the things that you don't authentically want and need, how can you do it with the bigger aspects of your life?

Take a look around your home. Do you have too much stuff? Do your walls need to be repainted? Do you keep broken things? Do you have ragged furniture? Get rid of things that you don't like. Kondo recommends starting with clothing, then books and papers, and leaving the sentimental stuff for last.

To be clear, it isn't your environment that creates peace or happiness. Were that the case, there would never be strife or warfare in beautiful settings. No one would be unhappy if they lived in a lovely place. However, when we are seeking to be more in touch with our hearts, things like flowers and candles help us settle into the stillness that lies at our center. They evoke what's *already true of us*. They can create a sense of the sacred in the physical realm we reside in that honors our inner divinity.

Treating your home and other surroundings as sacred spaces calms the turbulent sea of thoughts in your mind, as does being in nature.

Back to Nature

Being in nature is healing and helps us get back to our essence. We find ourselves feeling grounded in nature, calmer in nature, and more in touch without our authentic core in nature. Perhaps this is because nature has a timeless element. Although unprecedented global changes may soon threaten this feeling of stability we've heretofore felt in nature, for now the ocean provides a comforting rhythm. The tides have been rolling in and out for thousands of years. Mountain peaks and ancient forests give us a sense of something greater than ourselves and the depressing news headlines of the day. The smell of pine needles and the trickle of water from creeks or the rush of water as it flows down a river can lull us into a sweet peace. Many of us feel more relaxed and are able to breathe easier in the wilds of nature than in the controlled chaos of urban environments.

One reason nature is so healing is that the air in the mountains, at the beach, and near waterfalls is filled with negative ions—odorless, tasteless molecules, that, according to health writer Denise Mann, "produce biochemical reactions that increase levels of the mood chemical serotonin, helping to alleviate depression, relieve stress, and boost our daytime energy."[4] Thus, we can retreat to nature, with its antidepressant qualities, to sort out what's deeply important in our lives and allow ourselves to connect with our untamed hearts.

There are many reasons we feel calmer in natural settings. Nature is beautiful. Natural landscapes are easy on the eyes. The verdant green of the plants and trees, the colorful swatches of flowers, the healing energy in the rocks, and the glistening water makes us feel good. We experience the perfection of the divine creation, and it helps us remember our own. We also tend to slow down in nature and begin tapping into our natural rhythms and pace.

If you're feeling disconnected from yourself, spend at least thirty minutes in a natural setting, preferably one that has a maximum of nature and a minimum of other people. If you are in a time of serious soul searching, or at a crossroads, and need to make some big decisions, more significant time in nature may be beneficial. Giving yourself this gift will allow you to come back to yourself and get clarity on any challenges you are facing and make more grounded decisions.

Don't Just Do Something, Sit There

Another way to connect with your deeper essence is to meditate. Meditation is the most powerful way to calm the mind and tap into your inner guidance. It promotes feelings of wellbeing and heightened awareness.

Researchers are finding that meditation increases mental and physical health.[5] Along with reducing stress and anxiety, it helps banish negative thoughts and lift a depressed mood.[6] Other benefits include a reduction of insomnia and a lowering of blood pressure. There are even indications that meditation can lessen your cravings for nicotine and other addictive substances. Plus, it costs you nothing except the investment of your time. Investing 5–15 minutes of your day can bring you greater mental clarity, stress reduction, and positive health benefits, while at the same time opening to your heart's desires and innate wisdom.

You don't need to be part of any religious or spiritual tradition to meditate. You don't need to sit in an uncomfortable position without moving for long periods.

You can start by sitting quietly for just five or ten minutes each day. While you're sitting, try to be as still as possible. Refrain from scratching or fidgeting if you are able. Don't be alarmed if you have a lot of thoughts—that's normal. Don't judge them. In fact, don't pay them any attention. Simply allow them to arise without fighting them. You'll find that just by observing yourself, your usual mental chatter will gradually dissipate of its own accord.

If you wish, increase the amount of time you sit in meditation. The more frequently and the longer you meditate, the more significant the effects on your mind will be. Your thoughts will continue to slow down. Imagine your brain is a glass of water. Each thought you have is like air blown through a straw into this glass of water, creating bubbles. The more thoughts, the more bubbles. Once you start meditating, it's as if the flow of air through the straw lessens and your thoughts gradually die down. No more bubbles, only still water.

Allow me to share with you just how powerful meditation can be. I'm not suggesting you necessarily do this, but I once attended a ten-day silent meditation retreat. We meditated for a minimum of five hours a day and could do up to ten hours if we wished. The rest of the time, we remained silent. We also refrained from reading, writing, and exercising, which meant we really were alone with our thoughts. I won't lie to you, at times it was dreadfully boring. Though they told us we were undertaking a sort of mental surgery, clearing out our mind, it honestly felt like nothing was happening.

When I arrived home, my wife at the time and a friend of ours wanted the three of us to go for ice cream. As I was driving, they suddenly burst out laughing. "What's so funny?" I asked. They were laughing because I was driving under the speed limit. Apparently, I wasn't in a hurry, whereas usually I was *always* in a hurry. They even told me to speed up!

When we reached our destination and entered the ice cream parlor, I had no idea what flavor I wanted. On the retreat, we were told that meditation would stop cravings. As I mulled over my choices, I realized I didn't even want ice cream. Later that evening, while eating dinner, I noticed how good the food tasted. Typically, I just wolfed my food down, seeing eating as more of a necessity. Now, I was savoring everything. I not only tasted each carrot, I felt the texture. It was the same with the cucumbers, avocados, lettuce. It was like I had taste buds for the first time in my life.

Along with increased awareness, I also lost something. The critical voice in my head that was always judging things and providing negative commentary 24/7 was gone. I listened for it, but it wasn't there. In its place was a quietness, a stillness, marked by a feeling of peace and contentment. This was a huge contrast from before. At thirty-three years of age, I couldn't remember a day when that inner critic wasn't active—and now it was gone. Hallelujah!

Quite spontaneously, I also stopped cursing—just like that. My language cleaned up because there was no need to cuss, since nothing pushed my buttons. Profane language suddenly seemed unnecessarily harsh. For several months after the retreat, not a single swear word crossed the threshold of my lips.

Ten days of silent meditation had shifted my whole being. By becoming still, all of the busyness, mental clutter, and emotional turmoil that generally blocked my awareness of my naturally peaceful and contented self, had evaporated, leaving just my essence. When I am living in my heart, my essence is naturally joyful and upbeat.

As with aerobic exercise, to keep receiving the benefits of meditation, you have to do it regularly. It's one of the most powerful tools to help you stay grounded, balanced, clear, and connected to yourself and your innate wisdom. You're going to need all that to move through the changes you'll find yourself making.

Take a Walk on the Deeper Side

Every year thousands of seekers, or *pilgrims,* as they are called, are drawn to a 500-mile path in Spain is known as *El Camino de Santiago* ("the Way"). They come for various reasons—religious tradition, spiritual inspiration, solace, escape from their current lives—in search of inner direction, seeking deeper meaning, to mark a time of transition, as a chance to heal their wounds, as well as to experience adventure and a new sense of freedom. Whatever a particular individual's reason, the underlying purpose of walking the Camino is to connect more deeply with themselves.

When you're walking, you're more likely to be present—if for no other reason than that if you zone out as you walk, you're likely to trip over a curb, step in dog poop, or wander into the path of a vehicle. When you're walking mindfully, you feel your toes in your shoes, you enjoy the breeze on your face, and you smell the jasmine blooming or the scent of orange blossoms. You can even feel when you're walking by water because of the change in temperature on your skin. Your senses are awake, and therefore so are you! No longer the living dead, you are in the right state to listen to your heart.

A simple walk can help you reset your being, enabling you to center and come back to yourself. Walking helps you get into the flow of your being. As you walk, you become more present in your body where you can tap into how you really feel. Walking mindfully can also help you tap into your own cadence. All of this helps you connect with your self on a deeper level.

You might try going for a walk when your only agenda is to walk and let yourself be guided in the direction your heart wants to go. If you feel like turning down one street or another, do it. If you want to stop and smell the roses, take a moment to do so. If you want to pick up a rock and examine it, pick up a rock. If you want to sit on a stump or a park bench, have a seat. Take a meandering kind of walk where you just let your heart lead the way.

I recommend doing this out in nature because it's easier to listen to your heart, since at least your physical body is present, even if your thoughts aren't. Because nature is a divine canvas, the wild heart of God, it calls us back to the wholeness that's our essence. Nature is never confused about what it is.

Having said this, you can also do this exercise in a suburban or urban area if need be. The objective is to slow down and let yourself *feel* your way through the walk. Allow yourself to stop, be curious, and notice what's around you. Getting into your senses facilitates getting into your heart. What sights, smells, or sounds do you notice as you walk?

Once you've connected to your deeper essence, it's time to begin noticing your intuitive nudges. The little impulse from your heart that speaks to you. For example, something inside of you urging you to take a particular course of action. A message from the intuition usually can be a felt sense or a gut feeling about a person or a situation. It is unlikely that your intuition will speak to you in words—although everybody is wired differently, and some people do receive intuitive messages in whole sentences.

Noticing your intuitive nudges is step four in the hearticulation process. In the next chapter, we will explore these nudges as a way your deeper self speaks to you.

INVITATION

Take a look at the practices for connecting with your deeper self and pick one to focus on each week until you've had a chance to do them all. For example, this week you might choose to begin clearing the clutter in your home, letting go of things that no longer fit or bring you joy. The following week you might begin by bringing home a new plant or picking out a piece of art or another special object that will bring beauty or joy into your home. After you've cleansed and beautified your space, consider sitting in meditation and embracing moments of silence and stillness. Notice what comes up for you as you begin to quiet the body and mind. Or after beautifying your space and clearing the clutter, you may decide to take some time out to be in nature. Notice if you feel more or less connected to your authentic self as you begin to interact mindfully with your physical surroundings.

CHAPTER FIVE

Honor Your Intuitive Nudges

"The intuitive mind is a sacred gift and the rational mind is a faithful servant. We have created a society that honors the servant and has forgotten the gift."
—Bob Samples

Have you ever had a hunch or an intuitive nudge? It's just a simple inner knowing. Something tells you to do something or not do something. It's like a voice inside that seems to be trying to bring your attention to something. For example, you have a sense that you should turn down a certain street, go to a particular store, turn on the radio, or call a friend. Do you listen? Do you follow that nudge, or do you ignore it? What happens when you follow it? Have you called the friend and discovered that they were just thinking about you? Have you taken a different route home and discovered that there was a huge accident on the way you usually travel, or that on the alternative route you've driven, you pass by a new restaurant you'd like to try?

I've found that when I followed those nudges and go to a particular store or café, I often run into someone I haven't seen in a while. I love that.

Have you had bigger nudges? Has the voice within and the inner knowing tried to get your attention about bigger things? Have you felt the need to take your car in and found out perhaps that something was off with your engine and needed to be repaired? Have you ever felt like something was off with someone and discovered later that they weren't being truthful with you? Have you ever felt the need to start looking for a job and then found out that your company was laying people off?

Our inner wisdom guides us if we listen to what it is urging us to do.

There are some circumstances when we don't listen or find it harder to listen and follow the nudges of our intuition. I remember blowing past one of those intuitive nudges. After a long workweek at the prison where I worked as a counselor, I'd scheduled a therapeutic massage at a spa I'd been going to for fifteen years. The place was professional, and I'd always had good experiences, so I didn't know how to respond when the massage therapist came out to greet me in the waiting room and something inside of me said, *Don't go.* I couldn't explain it. There was nothing odd about the massage therapist. She seemed normal enough and I'd already paid for the session in advance, as was the spa's policy.

I ignored the inner voice and went to the room, disrobed and got on the massage table. As the woman started to massage my arm, it felt like she yanked my shoulder out of its socket. I screamed in pain. I'd never screamed in a massage before.

"Oh, that hurt!" I said.

She didn't apologize.

To the contrary, she challenged me and tried to justify the pain she'd just caused me as being good for me.

When I went home that night I noticed I had a giant bruise on my shoulder and I couldn't lift my arm. I took ibuprofen, but it didn't help. The next morning it hurt so bad I called in sick and had to cancel the psych class I was supposed to teach that evening. I called the spa and told them what happened and asked for my money back. They declined. They told me that the therapist said she hadn't done anything unusual in the massage.

Two days later I went to urgent care. The doctor looked at the bruise and said my muscles had been torn. He asked how I got the injury and I told him a massage. He was shocked. He told me I should file a claim. I took his advice and more pain medication.

I filed a claim and received my money back for the massage as well as two days' worth of wages. If I'd just listened to the intuition, that crazy hunch or nudge, and been willing to walk away from the $70 I'd prepaid for the massage, I would have saved myself a lot of pain and inconvenience. Instead, I ignored the urging voice, trying to spare me, because I was too embarrassed to break a social contract based on intuition alone and walk away.

Have you had a similar experience? Are you getting nudges now that you're ignoring?

Relationships are another area where many of us find it difficult to listen to our inner knowing. I've had several couples come to me for marriage therapy where one of the partners is convinced that the other is having an affair. Their spouse adamantly denies it. Sometimes in the course of therapy the truth of the affair comes out. Sometimes the spouse comes out. Other times, the couples' work goes in circles until the couple stops coming to therapy. Months later, I'll hear back from one of the spouses that their intuition was spot on: their husband or wife was having an affair.

I've also seen this with clients who are dating. They get a vague sense that the person they are dating is not being completely honest with them, but they ignore those feelings because there are so many other wonderful characteristics about the person. Months later, they discover that the person is married, an alcoholic, lying about their job, using them for money, or something else that would have been a deal breaker if the person had been honest with them.

One client of mine had a boyfriend ask her for $5,000, claiming that his father had a stroke and he needed the money to pay the hospital bill or his father would stop receiving medical care. She gave him the money, and not surprisingly, never heard from him again.

Shockingly, I've seen this scenario go down with many good-hearted women and men from all backgrounds who are intelligent and educated. The common denominator is that they're not listening to their inner guidance and they're putting other people's needs first.

This is a far cry from being true to yourself.

When the Hero Takes the Fall

Another area where we may fail to listen to our inner knowing and defer to another is with the people we respect. They can be bosses, financial or legal experts, medical professionals, healers, community leaders, psychics, ministers, priests, gurus, and so on. People we look up to. People who we believe know more than us. It can be so challenging to listen to your inner guidance when it is running contrary to that of the people in your life whom you admire.

There are some amazing teachers out there who can teach us how improve our finances, be more successful in business, lose weight, connect more deeply with God, or increase our chances of finding our soulmates. However, there are also people who consciously and intentionally create fear in you to manipulate you into giving them your money. From companies who create catastrophic car wreck commercials to sell their products to psychics who create fear in you so that you'll keep working with them to remove your bad karma—fear sells products.

Have you ever become enthralled with someone? Have you ever looked up to an athlete or a musician? Have you ever followed a guru or a community leader only to find out that they don't walk their talk? It's not always clear who is there for your good and who is there to exploit you. Some of these folks aren't all bad or good. Sometimes what they're offering is super helpful, it's just not the right investment for you at this time in your life. Social convention can ask us to set aside our personal feelings or concerns in order for the group to get along. We commonly adhere to our parents', elders', or teachers' instructions at the expense of our own well-being.

I heard one story from a client about a charismatic professor in a religious university who raped her during his office hours. She told a classmate who refused to believe her. She told her parents and they told her not to report it, as it would hurt the community because of this man's status. Word of her accusations spread, and she was summarily ostracized. Although, one by one, a handful of other female students approached her and told her that they had been raped by him too. When they had reported it to the educational administrators, whose interest was in protecting the school from scandal, they had been talked out of pressing charges.

To please her parents, she never contacted the police. She ended up dropping out of school and coming to me to help her deal with her depression.

It takes great courage to speak your truth. The whole #METOO movement has shown us how too many women have held back on reporting their experiences and how powerful it is when rape and assault victims come forward together to challenge abuse, refusing to remain silent.

Sometimes your intuition is not warning you of extreme danger. You may just be getting an inkling that something is askew with a professional you interact with. Maybe this person's eye is not on the ball right now for personal reasons that they are trying unsuccessfully to keep compartmentalized and you sense it without understanding why. Or maybe something doesn't feel right about the suggestions of your financial planner and you discover that they're trying to sell you products you don't need. Or maybe you always felt good tithing to your church or synagogue until one day you don't. Suddenly you find yourself feeling uncomfortable writing that check and putting it in the basket. A few months later you discover that the treasurer at your house of worship is being brought up on charges of embezzlement. You knew something was off beforehand, but you just couldn't put your finger on what it was, so you chose not to trust yourself.

Or perhaps, you did trust yourself when something like this happened. You honored the intuitive nudge inside of you and found out later that your hunch was correct.

If you want to honor your true self, then begin to listen to the nudges of your intuition even in the absence of proof. You don't have to accuse anyone of anything, just exercise your right to choose. You can keep your reasons private. When you take an action that honors what you know on an intuitive level, you are connecting with your authentic core and this will serve you on your path.

By heeding your inner nudges you'll become ready to connect with your heart's desires—a step you'll experience in the next chapter which is the crux of the hearticulation process.

INVITATION

Open your journal and write down some intuitive hunches you've had in the past. Did you follow them? What happened, if so? Did you ever have intuitive hunches that you didn't follow? What happened then? This week notice any intuitive hunches you have and follow them. See what outcomes that creates for you. Notice if you feel more or less connected to your authentic self as you take your intuitive hunches seriously. Notice if you feel more in alignment with life as you follow your hunches or nudges. Do you find more synchronicities happening? Do you find yourself making wiser choices?

CHAPTER SIX

The Heart of the Matter

"Above all else, be the heroine of your life, not the victim."
—Nora Ephron

What would you do if you knew you couldn't fail? *What would you do if you only had a year to live?* I love these kinds of questions because they get us to move through some of our internal blocks and begin to daydream. As we do, we go beyond culturally perceived limitations to imagine something more for ourselves. Like Oprah Winfrey, who at a young age decided she was going to be a newscaster, despite the institutionalized racism and sexism that existed around her. She saw past it. And now, she's Oprah. Last name optional.

To state your preference requires you to find *your voice*. For life to manifest your dream, you've got to be able to express what's important to you, and you need to be clear and explicit. The universe needs to know what matters to you, what you are passionate about, what you love.

At this point, if you've followed the steps I've laid out for you, you've opened your heart, connected with your deeper self, and begun to follow your intuitive hunches.

This brings us to hearticulating, a process that includes identifying and articulating your heart's desires. *Hearticulation* is a process of deep inquiry into the experiences you want to have, the contributions you want to make, and the dreams you want to come true. When you hearticulate, you articulate to yourself and others what really matters to you.

There are a few important actions to take to prepare yourself.

Clear physical clutter. Before you begin this part of the process of *hearticulation,* begin by clearing space for yourself physically. You might begin by cleaning up your living quarters. Clear off a desk. Dust. Take those old clothes you haven't worn in three years out of your closet and drop them off at your local Goodwill. You'll find that once you've removed the physical clutter in your life, you'll have more success at relaxing (instead of stressing), which will help you enter the stillness that allows you to hear your heart.

Clear mental space. As I discussed in the chapter on connecting more deeply with yourself, you can use practices like meditation to calm the mind and create more mental space for yourself—so you can dream, think, and plan.

Be intentional. Once you've cleared your mental and physical space, you next want to create an environment that supports you in tapping into your heart's desires. Grab a notebook and pen, light a candle, and maybe put on some mood music. Sit down someplace you won't be disturbed for at least fifteen minutes, though an hour would be ideal. You are making time for your dreams to bubble up so that you can connect with your heart's desires.

Unleash your dreams. Now you are ready to begin dreaming in earnest. Start by filling in the blanks to these statements:

- "It would be really fun to . . ."
- "If I had an abundance of time and money I would..."
- "In my lifetime I want to . . ."

Write down all the things you want to do in your lifetime. Don't judge yourself, just write. Keep writing all the things you want to do until you run out of ideas. This doesn't mean that you will do them all, or that you need to do them all. This is just an opportunity to let the doors of your heart open and imagine your life out of the box. Allow yourself to connect deeply with your heart's desires.

You can find some downloadable worksheets that will help you hearticulate your heart's desires on my website: FollowYourCourageousHeart.com.

Everyone's dream is going to look different. One individual dreams of backpacking through the jungles of South America and apprenticing with shamans. Another of keeping his day job while taking art lessons in the evening. Yet another wants to quit her day job and open a bookstore café where she works for herself and sets her own hours.

Identify your must list. Once you've spent considerable time engaging in your inquiry of the heart—perhaps even multiple dreaming sessions—go over your list and begin to identify the things that matter most to you. Start by identifying your *must list*. This list includes all the things that *must* occur in your lifetime for you to be able to look back on your life from a rocking chair in old age and have a feeling of completeness. If you do these things, you will have answered your heart's calling and served your soul (and perhaps your sole) purpose.

My client Monica knew her heart's calling was to be an alternative healer, even though she was a very successful and well-paid nurse. My client Rachel was a very successful ad executive, but she had gone to film school and was not going to be content until she was following her true calling to make movies. My client Brad's list included getting married, having a family, and participating in work that made a positive difference in the world. My client Nancy's must list included exploring the world. Many of the items on her list involved travel experiences—everything from going on an intensive cross-country bike trip through France to riding horses in Mongolia. It also included creating a loving relationship with a partner and being part of a supportive community.

What's on your must list?

Tighten your focus. Once you've created your overall must list for your entire lifetime, mark which items you particularly want to focus on in the next one to three years. Of these items, winnow the list down further to the top three things you want to focus on and put them on a separate piece of paper. These top three goals will become your *courageous heart list*.

Once you've created your courageous heart list you may feel overwhelmed trying to figure out where to begin. And that's why I encourage you to take baby steps.

Generate your baby steps. Begin generating baby steps you could take toward your dream. You'll want to generate a list of steps that makes each top goal doable. For example, if you decide one of your dreams is to hike the Incan trail to Machu Picchu, some baby steps you could take to reach this goal might include: going online and looking up the best times to hike there, researching the best adventure companies to book with, finding out what kind of shape you need to get in, and knowing what the cost would be. Also, practical steps like pricing airline tickets, reading reviews on books about the Inca Trail, and learning more about the experience and how to prepare.

If your dream is to learn how to play the harp, perhaps begin looking around for harpists who teach.

Start learning about harps and pricing them. Does it make more sense to buy a harp new or used? Does it make sense to lease one from a music store until you figure out whether this is something you really enjoy, or more of a whim? In Chapter 7, "Take Baby Steps," I'll share some ideas with you on how to break down your dreams into baby steps that lead to specific actions you can take in the direction of your dreams.

Some things may not turn out to be as much fun as you imagined. My hobbies are a prime example of this. I really wanted to take a fencing class. Upon attending my first class, however, I found it less spirited than I imagined it would be, and fencing lost my attention.

On the other hand, some of your heart's desires may become part of a new way of life, experiences and activities you'll want to return to again and again. When I first traveled to Italy in 2003, the trip was life changing. A dream awakened in me to spend three weeks in Venice on a personal writing retreat. This was a big dream. I planned the trip for 2006. During those three intervening years, I saved up not only enough money but also sufficient vacation days. Six months before my trip, I researched inexpensive places to stay, rented an apartment in the Santa Croce District, and bought my ticket to the Marco Polo Airport. This experience liberated me from my daily routine and what I believed was possible for me. The trip made an indelible impression on my soul, with the result that my life has never been the same. Since then I've made it a must to travel to Italy regularly to reconnect with myself and feed my Italian soul.

My client William dreamed of leaving his job behind and moving to the country. His life in the city, with a big house and a big mortgage, might have impressed many, but trying to keep up with the Joneses and the lifestyle expected of someone in his profession, stole his joy. He wanted to wake up every morning to the sight of pine and maple trees and go to sleep every night under a canopy of stars. I worked with him to hearticulate what was really important to him, and then we were able to help him take the steps to create his new reality.

One couple I was coaching wanted a total life makeover. They were both professionals living in a two-bedroom home in a polluted, urban area, each working forty-plus hours a week and languishing over the fact that their nanny spent more time with their children than they did. They dreamed of moving to a smaller town and living a simple life, although they had no idea how they could finance this dream. Had money not been an issue, they would have moved after the birth of their first child.

As their coach, I assured them their dream was attainable. Since they wanted a total makeover, we were careful not to compromise any aspect of their dream as we began exploring options. Within six months, they found the perfect home to rent in their dream location. One parent was able to telecommute full time, with occasional visits to the office. The other was able to get a job in their new hometown. They attained their dream and are now living in a large home with a big backyard in a small town with fresh country air. The community has met all of their needs, including a weekly organic farmer's market. They didn't have to sacrifice anything. They only had to let go of their limited belief that they couldn't really live their dreams. Two years later, they contacted me to thank me and tell me that they had realized another one of their dreams: opening up their own business. I was so happy for them. They said, "You showed us that dreams really can come true."

We'll dive deeper into how to generate and order your baby steps in part two of the book.

Part Two

Take Back Your Life

CHAPTER SEVEN

Take Baby Steps

*"Faith is taking the first step even when you
don't see the whole staircase."*
—Martin Luther King, Jr.

N ow that you've hearticulated your dreams and
desires, you may want to leap toward your
dreams. When we leap to make huge changes that
fully immerse us in pursuing our dreams it can be
exhilarating. Over years of choosing to listen to my
authentic self, I've learned a lot about the process of
transition, how to take big leaps, and stay courageous, and I
understand what kind of dramatic change that creates in my
life. But I must admit that sometimes taking big leaps can
leave me feeling overwhelmed. These days I prefer a
steadier and more measured approach toward the
realization of my dreams.

Sometimes we do need to take leaps of faith and trust
that the net will appear. However, our leaps of faith can be
hard on us—emotionally taxing. If we don't know how to
be with the free fall, we might panic.

If you're going to leap be sure you have solid support. You need to prepare for the leap. You have to engage regularly and without fail in mental practices that keep your mind focused on the direction you want to take your life. You have to engage in practices that create an inner state of trust and faith to stay emotionally and psychologically on course and not give up. You need to have a support team and be very intentional about creating massive disruption in your life. Otherwise, if you go too fast and overwhelm yourself you may become reluctant to make changes, frozen, and freaked out. That's not exactly empowering.

So, let's talk about how to set yourself up for success by working with baby steps.

The ideal approach for the majority of my clients is to build an imaginal bridge from where they are now to where they want to be, and then take baby steps to cross that bridge. Baby steps allow us to slowly develop new habits and patterns, and to experience and celebrate successes along the way. This is important!

My client Melinda had a great idea for a consumer product. She had to take a lot of steps to create her product, including finding someone to develop the prototype, testing it out, researching her market, finding a factory that could manufacture the product, then promoting it, and selling to customers.

Another client, Demi, a hairdresser, wanted to open her own hair salon. She had to find a building in a location that was conducive to people having their hair styled. To pay for the building, as well as the mirrors, sinks, and barber chairs to fill the space, she not only had to commit her own money but also identify investors. Then she had to hire a crew to renovate the space, as well as hire support staff and other stylists, along with promoting her salon. This was a huge undertaking and she needed to have immense faith in herself. Demi took the steps needed and created a gorgeous, successful salon.

Do you have a great idea for a product or a business? What steps could you take to start moving in the direction of your dreams? What would you have to believe about yourself to take the first step?

Baby steps help us begin to chunk complex actions together. *Chunking* is a psychological term used to describe the process of how we are able to remember information more easily when like information is managed together. Taking baby steps allows you to chunk sequences together. This behavior creates new habits and muscle memory. As you are taking these baby steps, you are engaging in mental and physical rehearsal of new behaviors in a way that allows you to slide easily into change. Because of the pace of baby steps, habits are gradually created and the changes feel easy and congruent, naturally becoming a part of your new identity.

Below you will find some examples of how to use baby steps and chunking. These examples will show you how you can implement a focused action plan so you can begin moving forward on your dreams and desires. You can return to your hearticulation list and begin creating your action plan and building on the vision of living your beautiful, authentic life.

Baby Steps to Health and Fitness

Let's say you want to get into shape and care for your physical wellbeing. Perhaps your goal is to go to the gym three days a week and you've either never done this before or it's been a long time. You're going to want to break this down into doable baby steps where you can feel successful every step of the way. You'd want to begin by preparing for the gym. One way to do this is to give yourself a week to take the first step, which might be finding and signing up at a gym. Your second week, your next baby step might be to buy gym clothes. Your third week, your baby step might be to buy tennis shoes.

This gives you three weeks to find a gym, enroll, and get clothes and shoes to work out in. You may find that you can do all these things easily in one week or you may find that you need more time. If you discover that you're procrastinating, then having an accountability buddy could help or you may need to adjust your expectations for yourself. Whatever you decide, it's important that you continue to take steps in the direction of your dreams and celebrate yourself every step of the way. Imagine the kind of encouragement and praise a toddler gets every time it takes a step when learning to walk. You deserve support as well. Shower yourself with kindness and praise!

In your fourth week, you may want to pick three mornings that you will go to the gym before work and schedule these times in your calendar and/or set a reminder alarm on your phone.

On the first day, your goal might be to set the alarm for the gym, get up, and put on your gym clothes. Going to the gym is optional. On the second day, your baby steps might be to set the alarm, get up when the alarm goes off, put on your gym clothes, and drive to the gym. Now you know what that feels like and how much time it takes.

On the third workout day, your baby steps might be to set the alarm, get up when the alarm goes off, put on your gym clothes, drive to the gym, and walk inside the gym. You could leave after that or while you're there, look around. You might even try one of the machines—but only if you feel like it.

Every step you take on your action plan is a rehearsal for the next, which is a means of changing your patterns and beginning a lifestyle and identity change. By taking baby steps you're beginning to chunk the steps together and experiencing success. If you find yourself overwhelmed by these steps, again slow it down and go back to the last step you had success with. Consider getting an accountability buddy or a coach who can support you.

Take time to warm up. Don't overdo the exercise. Getting in shape is a marathon, not a sprint. You are building a new routine to last a lifetime. In this example, you are building a whole new body and way of being. Go lightly and move incrementally. Don't move so fast that you injure yourself and then need to go back to square one until you heal.

If you find yourself breezing by these baby steps, of course, you can move ahead, just make sure you are creating consistency. Enjoy each moment of achieving your goals. Feeling good about your efforts is the key to being successful, as it will create the intrinsic motivation to continue. Celebrate your successes, otherwise as you move from goal to goal, your achievements will feel empty.

By the end of the first month, if you continue with the steps outlined above, you will find yourself at the gym three times a week. Once you've established this routine, you can start building on your aerobic exercise by getting on the treadmill or some other cardio machine or class for 10–30 minutes depending on your level of fitness.

By the sixth week, you can add additional time to your workouts, which should now be a part of your routine three times a week. This is what baby steps can do for us. They can gradually ease us into creating positive changes in our lives. Again, if you find yourself blasting through these steps, that's great; however, remember the point is to set yourself up for success and self-acknowledgment along the way, so that these steps stick.

Baby Steps to Build Your Own Business

Many of my coaching clients want to start their own businesses but feel overwhelmed by the process. Perhaps you've wanted to do this too. Starting your own business can seem daunting and overwhelming. Where do you begin? Baby steps!

You'll need to find ways to chunk starting your business into baby steps. Imagine a piece of paper with lines numbered from 1–50. Each line represents one week (a year's worth of efforts, with two weeks off for a vacation). In this scenario, with a focus on creating your own business, you will see how each action step per week allows you to meet your goal by year's end.

For example, Week 1, decide what kind of business you want to create. Week 2, buy a book on how to start a business. Week 3, read the book. Week 4, decide if your business will be brick and mortar or online. If brick and mortar, begin looking for a space to rent or buy to house it.

Week 5, have coffee with a business owner and ask about how he or she started his or her business. Week 6, get a mentor through the Small Business Administration or contact someone you know who has a business and ask if he or she'd be willing to mentor you. Week 7, decide on a name for your business. Week 8, file your business name with the county and list your business DBA ("doing business as") notification in a newspaper.

Week 9, purchase the URL for your business's website. Week 10, hire someone to begin building your website. Week 11, secure a physical location for your business or your office and sign that lease. Week 12, get business cards, and so forth.

Again, notice how the pace works for you. If you decide that you need to carry steps over from the previous week, don't sweat it. If you want to leave spaces every other week to give yourself more time to complete your baby steps, no problem. Do it.

Do you see how creating specific baby steps makes your dreams doable?

This strategy also works for accomplishing dream projects, like writing a master's thesis, a novel, or a children's book. Baby steps also can be used to buy a house, remodel a house, learn an instrument or a language, relocate to another city, start a new profession, return to school, build a community, make new friends, change a habit, and so much more. Taking one step at a time, you'll baby step your way to a life you love.

Baby Steps to Change the World

Taking baby steps can help you transform the world. Let's say one of your big dreams in life is to create transformational change on a social issue. An issue that I was passionate about was marriage equality. In 1997, when I became committed to changing the laws for same-sex couples to be able to marry, it wasn't legal anywhere in the world. I began forming committees and attending meetings with others. We bought clipboards and pens and stood on street corners a few days a month asking people to sign their names on a paper that read: "I support the right for same-sex couples to marry." It was a piece of paper with nothing but an affirmation of support and a place for people to write their names and email addresses. It had no legal significance. It was a baby step in the direction of creating support for the marriage equality movement.

My friends and I created non-binding resolutions (other pieces of paper that stated an affirmation of support for same-sex marriage) and we attended human rights council meetings in different cities in California where we asked these committees to vote in favor of this statement. We sat in these meetings while people on human rights committees debated whether or not all people deserve the human right to marry. Often, the nonbinding resolutions passed by only one vote (four to three).

Even though these non-binding resolutions had no legal power to change anything, they created social change by engaging people in conversations and hearing why marriage equality was as important to lesbians, gays, bisexuals, and transgender individuals, as it was to heterosexual couples.

We took the baby steps of traveling from city to city and finding local people who were willing to organize in their community and be a spokesperson on the issues. We called these people Marriage Equality Chapter Leaders. We then trained them and brought them together through the internet with our other chapter leaders across the state. This was the pre-Facebook era. It was pre-Twitter. Both these social networks launched in 2006. Our volunteer webmaster, Sean Conklin, and I sat down one November afternoon to create a program that would allow us to create a system that linked chapter leaders together, an email program for our members, and a way for chapter leaders to log in and get access to the mailing list of people in their areas. We did this because it was also the pre-Mail Chimp and Constant Contact era. We didn't yet have communication tools that organizers take for granted now.

Little by little we created a state-wide web, and then a national web, of leaders and members. By having a nationwide network of marriage equality supporters and leaders we were able to create synchronized events: marriage license counter asks in February, Tax Day rallies in April, *Get Engaged* educational campaigns, marriage equality booths and contingents in regional pride celebrations, and marriage equality *Day of Decision* events to celebrate the passage of marriage equality laws in other countries and states as they were passed. We mobilized our network to demonstrate against the injustice of being denied our human rights anytime states passed laws *against* same-sex marriage too.

Every baby step helped us to educate people about why marriage equality was a civil rights issue. Each baby step introduced more and more people to same-sex couples and why we needed their support. The whole series of baby steps helped change the tide and ultimately led to the sea change of support for equal marriage rights for same-sex couples.

Many LGBT people said they never thought they'd see marriage equality in their lifetimes. Tears ran down the faces of couples in their senior years who had been committed to their partners for decades. Even when confronting an issue as big, as controversial, and as seemingly improbable, if not impossible, as legalizing same-sex marriage nationwide, baby steps are proven to create change.

What issues are important to you? Climate change? Ending gun violence? Preventing sexual assault? Providing shoes to children, like it was to Blake Mycoskie, founder of Tom's Shoes? Ensuring girls get an education, like it was to Malala Yousafzai? Whatever you are passionate about, taking baby steps will create change. Like the old proverb "A journey of a thousand miles begins with one step," you just have to take that first baby step.

Blocks

Inevitably, as you begin moving in the direction of your dreams, obstacles will show up. Don't get discouraged. When we meet with blocks we are given the opportunity to refine and discern our desires. Do we really want the cabin in the mountains or would we rather have a house we could retire to in Palm Springs? Do we really want to travel to Peru and do *ayahuasca* or would a service trip to Guatemala bring more satisfaction?

Take a look at the blocks. Do your blocks have to do with a lack of money or other resources? If they do, this may require you to get creative as you look for ways to raise funds, such as comingling money or finding others who want to share in, or invest in your vision.

My young friend Luca wanted to build a computer from the ground up. He shared his vision with his family and friends. He let them know why he wanted to build his own unit and then shared with them the prices of each individual component. His uncle was particularly impressed by how he clearly articulated his dreams and goals at twelve years old. His family was excited to support his efforts and paid him to do odd jobs to help him raise money for his computer parts. Instead of giving gifts of presents on Christmas and for his birthday, they donated money to his build-a-computer fund. Within five months, Luca raised the funds needed to purchase and build his own computer.

If money is what's holding you back from creating your vision, see if you can enroll people who frequent Kickstarter, Patreon, Go Fund Me, or other crowd-funding sites. These communities can help you fund the creation of whatever it is you want to birth, whether it's a web-based TV series, an independent film, a documentary, a musical album, a novel, an audiobook, or something else.

Are the blocks related to other people in your life? When the blocks are other people, we may have to look at letting go of those people or of the idea of including those people in some aspects of our goals and dreams. For example, one of my workshop participants wanted to travel, but her husband was unable to get time off from work. She'd always dreamed of traveling through Europe with her husband. We worked together to help her find a way to pursue her dreams. She decided to take six weeks and go without him. She invited friends who had also always wanted to travel and were afraid to go by themselves. One friend flew over with her and then they parted ways. Another friend came the same day, and yet another met her a few days later in another country. She had the time of her life and even confided that she wished she'd had more unscheduled time to travel by herself. She returned home refreshed and with a new confidence in herself.

If your dream is to spend a year living at sea and your partner has terrible sea sickness, then living out the dream of traveling the oceans together may be more challenging. Would you be willing to experience your year at sea one month at a time over the next twelve years? Or would you be willing to shorten your sailing excursion to, for instance, three months? If not, would you be willing to accept that while you are at sea for a year your beloved may find himself or herself a landlubber back home? If long-term sailing is a real dream of yours and not shared by your beloved, maybe there's a mermaid or merman out there who would be an even better fit for you than your current partner. In which case, you're possibly holding yourself back by not taking that sailing trip and the chance to embrace greater happiness.

Are the blocks about time or other commitments? When the blocks to our dreams are a lack of time and or having to do with multiple commitments, we may need to look at how we can adjust, maybe spending less time on doing what we love or taking more time to get there. For example, if your dream is to get a college degree and you have children or family members to care for, you may need to start by taking one class a time. You may need to consider beginning with online college classes and then transferring your earned credits to a community college or university once you are able. And you may need to ask family members or friends for more support. Maybe you could do babysitting swaps with your kid's friends' parents when your school is on break. Maybe you need to look into hiring a nanny.

It can be painful when you have multiple commitments that are important to you. The thought of losing time with your kids may be equally as painful as not achieving your dream. However, finding a balance that allows you to be your whole self is going to feel rewarding in the end. My client Olivia sacrificed sleep and her need to be perfect at all of her endeavors so that she could go back to school for a master's degree. Olivia began grad school only three months after becoming a new mother.

Olivia gradually began letting go of the need to be an overachiever at work, learning to let other people begin to pull more weight, while also excusing herself from extracurricular activities with her colleagues and in her community. Olivia asked her family for support. Her sister, who was newly unemployed after taking time to travel, agreed to move in with Olivia for the first year of the baby's life, and helped her sister and brother in-law to raise their daughter. This was a great experience for everyone, bringing the sisters closer together.

While Olivia had less sleep, not only because of the newborn, but because she was staying up working on papers, her life was fuller in other ways. She quickly also realized that she didn't need to get straight As on every paper and class. A passing grade was all she needed to get her diploma.

Sometimes we find ourselves blocked by a lack of information or expertise. When the blocks have to do with not knowing enough, we can take a class, hire someone to help us, ask a friend who knows how to do what we want to do to show us how, or get a mentor. These days you can search just about any topic on Google and Bing and find ways to learn more. You can also watch YouTube instructional videos on almost any topic under the sun. And then, of course, you could also read a good, old-fashioned book.

Every step we take in the direction of our dreams keeps us vibrant and in alignment with our authentic essence. For every block we face, if we have a significant enough "why" motivating us, we'll find a way to move through it or around it.

INVITATION

Pick one of the top three items on your courageous heart list. Then, we'll do something similar to what was suggested in the section "Baby Steps to Build Your Own Business." Take out a piece of paper and pen, and number lines from 1–24. Write down twenty-four actions you can take to make this goal a reality. Choose the pace that works for you and begin. Decide whether you will take an action every week or every other week. The Universe wants to support you in bringing your dreams to life, however you have to play a part in the cocreation by taking regular steps in the direction of your dreams. You need to show up for class, book the airline tickets, schedule the coffee date, buy the URL, write the words on the page—whatever it is.

CHAPTER EIGHT

Move Through Fear

"Life shrinks or expands in proportion to one's courage."
—Anaïs Nin

To walk on fire, you need to be able to shift your focus away from what you're afraid of and keep it focused on where you want to go. As you walk, you keep your eyes straight ahead. You see where you want to be—on the other side of the coals. You don't look down. You don't look at the burning coals. It's helpful to have a chant like "I can do it" or "Yes! Yes! Yes!" to keep your mind focused and to distance yourself from your emotions and the feelings in your body. You don't let fear take up space in your body. If you do, you'll likely get burned.

I should know. I walked away from my first firewalk in 1999 with a painful burn blister. I was told after my walk that I should go to the "burn tent" where people like me, who "needed souvenirs" as proof of their experience, went for care and support. I was slightly amused by the notion of a souvenir because it resonated with me. The burn was a badge of courage to prove to myself that it was real, that I had walked on fire, and that there was no mistaking those coals were hot. It wasn't a trick. I had real reason to be afraid.

In the burn tent, one of the volunteers shared a story with a few of us about a young boy who had cancer and cured himself by visualizing Pac-Man eating up all the white blood cells in his body. The message was that we hold the power to change our realities if we choose to focus our minds over matter. Then the volunteer had us engage in several similar visualization practices to minimize our burns. Within two hours of my firewalk, the big blister was still there, but the pain from my blister was completely gone. I remember getting into the shower, grimacing that it would burn like hell when I turned the hot water on, like sunburns do. Even though the blister stayed with me for a full week, it never bothered me again. In fact, I've had sunburns that hurt longer than the firewalk blister. My mind didn't get it.

My second firewalk taught me another lesson about mind over matter, only this one was about the tricks the fearful mind plays on us. Nine months from the date of my first firewalk, I signed up to do a forty-foot firewalk (the first one was only eight feet long). The night of the forty-foot firewalk, I stood barefoot on the lush grass of the Waikoloa Marriot resort on Hawaii's big island.

As I waited in line for my turn to walk, I could smell the smoke from the fire and the coals. Suddenly, my feet began burning. Frightened, I stepped to the side of the line and looked down for the fugitive hot coal, but there was only grass.

How was this possible? I was standing on the cool grass, but my fearful mind had created an unreal experience that was causing me pain. My mind, of its own accord, had conditioned my body to feel pain when I experienced the combination of being barefoot, smelling smoke, and standing in line to do a firewalk.

I was blown away by the power of the mind to create fear and pain. I had to overcome this to complete the firewalk. This was no easy task. It was only when the fire line coach said "Show me what you're made of" that I was able to dig deep and muster unshakable determination and focus. In that moment, I was able to take that first step on to the bed of glowing reddish-orange coals, and then continue across for forty feet.

When I reached the other side, I checked my feet. They were unscathed. Not only had I walked across forty feet of hot coals, I had learned a profound lesson about how to move through fear.

Perhaps the fear *you* must face has more to do with putting yourself out in the world as you pursue your dreams. Your equivalent to a firewalk might be signing up for an open-mic night to read your poetry or perform a song you wrote. If you want to find the man or woman of your dreams, facing your fear might involve creating an online dating profile, going to a speed dating event, or participating in a singles' mixer.

Equally, your proverbial "firewalk" might be going to the local community college and registering for a class. These actions take courage, since they all involve you moving out of your comfort zone.

Assess Your Level of Risk

How far are you willing to move out of your comfort zone? How much risk are you willing to take? How much proverbial skin are you willing to put in the game?

I'm sure you've heard the phrase "Nothing ventured, nothing gained," which means that as we invest our time and resources into pursuing our heart's desires we have much to gain. It also means that we are exposing ourselves to some risk too. Whatever your dream is, living authentically and courageously doesn't necessarily mean you have to take radical risks or sell all your possessions. On the other hand, it doesn't preclude you from doing this if you really want to.

What does it mean to follow your heart? How do you know whether you are being reckless or foolish?

These are good questions without definitive answers. I can provide you with some guidance, but it's up to you to make the choices you need to make because you feel they are ultimately for your benefit. Much like going to a financial planner, you'll need to consider your adversity to risk.

If you are a person who doesn't like to take risks, you may want to begin following your heart in simple ways. For example, you could begin doing more enjoyable things on your weekends. You might try out new hobbies or outdoor sports or sign up for a class. If you've ever taken a class or seminar in investing or planning for your retirement you're likely familiar with levels of risk and benefit. As with a making a small financial investment you'll experience small, but gradual benefits with a minimal risk of loss. However, just by moving in this direction, you'll enrich your life. You may not feel completely gratified, but it will feel more pleasant than being disconnected from your passion.

If and when you are ready to take a medium amount of risk, investing more time, energy, and focus—and perhaps even money—in following your heart can open up opportunities to make some significant changes in your life. However, you simultaneously increase the possibility of experiencing some volatility. Taking medium risk means you're getting yourself out of your comfort zone. Perhaps you sign up to run a marathon, take an intensive workshop, or decide to travel.

On a larger scale, maybe your dream is becoming a standup comic, songwriter, screenwriter, or performer. You're doing the unexpected, which often involves saying no to certain social obligations or family expectations that would cause you to live less authentically. By being willing to risk losing the approval of others, you could even leave behind some of your relationships that don't meet you where you are.

When you are ready to unleash your courageous heart, a higher level of volatility and the risk that accompanies this journey are inevitable. Some will see following your heart to this degree as throwing caution to the wind. For this reason, it's not for the faint of heart, but the courageous.

High-risk ventures could include quitting your day job and starting your own business, or perhaps pursuing an entirely different career such as an artistic dream or a spiritual path. For example, you might decide to take a month to a year off to travel or live in another country—not because it's practical, but for no reason other than that you *want* to. It's one thing to take a job in another country for a year as a diplomat or consultant. Living in another country for a year because you wish to learn a second language, putting all your stuff in storage to live at an ashram in India, or backpacking across Europe for the experience is quite another.

High-risk investment means you could lose a lot and probably will. You might lose things you're better off without—things like the monotony of the daily grind, routines that have outlived their value, and especially the old ways of knowing yourself. You'll likely find yourself completely out of your comfort zone with little sense of security. When you risk your heart, you may experience rejection and failure, as the people you associate with will likely change. However, even when you feel like you're losing, you'll still be winning. By taking big risks, you'll experience a sense of aliveness—of really being invested in what you are doing instead of sitting on the sidelines. You will experience freedom like never before.

In a high-risk venture, *you* become responsible for your life. You use and develop muscles you didn't even know you had. Your sense of yourself expands. You lose who you were, or who you and others thought you were, which can be very intense. However, you create a new sense of yourself. If you go this route in your life, you will likely go places that your old self would never have traveled, meet people you would never have crossed paths with, and discovered things about yourself that you didn't know existed.

You may meet your *real* self out on the trail.

Face Your Fear, But Don't Focus on It

Fear is the number one obstacle that keeps people from following their hearts. We may be afraid of social rejection, failure, not having enough money, losing something or someone of value. We may be afraid of embarrassment, of looking stupid. We may be afraid of not being enough or being too much. We may be afraid of getting hurt or not being physically safe. We may be afraid of doing something that will negatively impact our ability to survive physically or financially.

This was the case for my client Monique. She owned a coffee shop and a portion of her café had a dedicated play area for parents and their children. Having a kid-friendly zone in her café was perfect for Monique when her children were young, however she now felt it was diminishing the ambience of her café. She felt it kept her from raising prices and raising the bar on her business. Monique wanted to up-level her café but felt paralyzed with worry that she would offend and lose her existing clientele if she made these changes . . . and then she'd go broke.

I had Monique envision what she wanted her café to look like. What was the feeling she wanted her clients to have when they were in the café? Also, I had her imagine her clients sharing their approval and excitement about the improvements she'd made to the café, rather than imagining clients expressing their disapproval. I encouraged her to picture the café filled with satisfied customers enjoying their beverages, this kept her focused on succeeding.

I wanted Monique to embody the feelings of success, so I invited her to imagine the good feelings she would feel once the changes she wanted to make were complete. How would it feel in her body when she walked into the updated café? By connecting with the future good feelings in her body Monique generated a sense of peace and certainty that she would be able to lean into as she began making the changes to her café.

Of course, every business needs a contingency plan in case something goes wrong. Monique needed to know that she had the wherewithal to survive negative appraisal by her clients and even her worst fears. I worked with Monique to help her create contingency plans. I had her imagine how she might deal with an irate mom expressing her upset with the changes to the café and how she'd handle it. I had her roleplay her response until it felt congruent for her to confidently address the imagined customer's concern. I wanted her to see that she could trust herself to effectively handle their concerns.

I also had Monique imagine what she would do if she had to close her café—her worst-case scenario. Monique recognized that if that happened she would begin by acknowledging herself for her years of running a successful business. She became clear that if her business did close she still had other interests and options. She could take a break. She could go on a vacation and then get a job. Then when she felt ready, and if she wanted to, she could start a new business. Ultimately, Monique realized that if her business closed it was because there was something more that wanted to transform in her life and not just the kids' play area of her café. She understood on a deeper level that if closing the business was called for, something better was likely to come into her life.

I didn't want Monique to spend more than 5 percent of her time imagining how she would cope with her business closing, just enough so that she knew she had the inner strength to get through such an experience with her contingency plans. The majority of my work with Monique was dedicated to having her focus on what she wanted to create and seeing herself succeeding.

Just like in the firewalk where I said, "I can do it!" as I crossed the hot coals, I worked with Monique to come up with empowering phrases and affirmations she could say to herself anytime she got stressed. Her statements were: "Lots of people love my café. The changes I'm making are improving my business. Everything is going to be okay. I'm doing a great job. Things always work out for the best."

Next, I worked with Monique to outline the actions needed to bring her new vision to life. She identified specific steps she would take to make the changes to improve her cafe. After doing this, I had her imagine that she was taking those steps. Mentally rehearsing the steps she needed to take made Monique feel more empowered. She could see herself moving through each action with ease and grace.

Once she had mentally rehearsed the steps, she was ready to take them. Since she was fearful of change we focused on her taking each step slowly. First, she let her customers know of the upcoming shifts that would be taking place. Next, she donated the toys and old furniture to charity. Then she went shopping for new furniture. She found a fashionable rug, a new couch, and comfortable armchairs.

It was important for Monique to feel that she wasn't alone in the process of change. I encouraged her to reach out to others. She organized a team of friends and staff to come to a painting and pizza party. They repainted the café and supported Monique in the transition. This created momentum and synergy, which I'll talk more about later in the book.

With new furnishings and fresh paint, the appearance of the café was dramatically altered. There was a new vitality to the place. The former kids' area was transformed into a cozy space for patrons to sip their tea or coffee, read books, and gather with friends.

Monique noticed an uptick in business within the first month. She began seeing new faces almost immediately. She realized that because there were no longer babies crying and unmodulated children's voices booming through the café, it was now a place of respite for the other patrons, as well as for her. She was no longer finding the occasional errant dirty diaper stuffed into a corner of the room or buried in a pile of toys. The café smelled better. It felt cleaner. She noticed that she felt a greater sense of clarity and focus. It wasn't that all of her problems were solved. However, it was a huge step forward in allowing herself to express her own needs as well as the business' needs to evolve.

Monique made sure to celebrate her success by documenting it in her journal and sharing before and after photos on her website and newsletter. By reviewing the transformation process she went through, she was able to reaffirm for herself what she could create by being willing to face and move through her fears.

As Monique had feared, some of her old clients, particularly mothers with young children, complained. A few of them even stopped coming. Because Monique had made contingency plans for this eventuality she was able to deal with her fears as they surfaced. She focused her energy on the compliments she received from patrons and on her growing new customer base.

At the end of the year, Monique compared her monthly earnings with earnings the previous year and realized that in the months since she'd closed the kids' area, she'd doubled her profits. Not only that, she'd also increased her sense of self-worth, which was priceless. If she'd focused on her fear of disappointing others, or on the prospect of losing devoted customers, it would have prevented her from taking action and she wouldn't have succeeded.

Is there a change you want to make and you are feeling stopped by fear? What views or attitudes would help you step out of your comfort zone and in the direction of your dreams?

Twelve Steps to Move Through Fear

Follow these twelve steps when you want to move forward and are feeling fearful.

1. Get clear on what you want. Take time to write out what you want. If writing it out doesn't work for you, ask a friend to interview you and describe your vision in as great of detail as possible. Remember to stay flexible, knowing that the right outcome will unfold perfectly even if it doesn't look exactly as you think it should.

2. Envision a successful outcome by focusing on what you want. Imagine your vision coming into fruition. See the goal complete. Picture yourself living your dream. For example, see yourself saying, "I do." See yourself cutting the ribbon on your new business. See yourself signing your published book at your favorite bookstore. Imagine yourself holding your baby. Picture yourself sipping coffee on the deck of your new home.

3. Embody the feelings of successfully moving through your fears. Feel into how it feels to be on the other side of your fears. How do you feel in your body? Do you walk differently? Is your posture better? Do you feel more relaxed? Is your breathing slower or faster? Do you feel a sense of peace or accomplishment? What does that feel like?

4. Create your contingency plan. Ask yourself what fears keep you from taking action on your goals. Then come up with a game plan or contingency plan for how you would deal with those situations if they were to occur. Most of the things we are afraid will happen don't, but we feel more comfortable and confident knowing we have taken preventive measures, so we know how we will react and respond if such things do happen. You want to know how you'd deal with your worst-case scenario situation. This is why we learn CPR, install smoke alarms, and own insurance of varying kinds. This allows us to feel confident if such situations arise.

But don't squander too much attention here. You don't spend the duration of your flight focusing on how to put on your oxygen mask in the case of a change of cabin air pressure. You briefly review the procedure before takeoff and then you focus on being at your destination. You imagine yourself enjoying Thanksgiving dinner with your family, walking on the beach, or visiting the Eiffel Tower. Spend the bulk of your attention on seeing yourself happy and succeeding.

5. Create empowering self-talk. Speak to yourself in an empowering way. Create a mantra, a phrase, or an affirmation that you can say to yourself to keep you focused on your goals and moving through your fears. "I got this. I can do it! I believe in myself. I trust life." Whatever statements help you feel empowered, employ those. And obviously, refrain from saying negative things.

6. Imagine yourself taking the steps to make it happen. What are the steps you need to take? Start a list. Write it down or dictate it into your phone. Then see yourself taking the steps to success. Engage in mental rehearsal. See yourself confronting a difficult person or situation. Imagine yourself confidently asking for a raise. See yourself making that pitch or proposal with confidence and having it received with enthusiasm. Do it over and over again until you feel comfortable and confident.

7. Start taking baby steps in the direction of your dreams. Begin taking the steps toward your dream or goal slowly and mindfully. Don't do more than you can handle or you will overwhelm yourself.

8. Get support. Confide in one or two people who are supportive and believe in you. In Chapters 14 and 15, you'll learn how to surround yourself with supportive people.

9. Have a strategy for dealing with your fear. If you find yourself freaking out, get control of your mind. Stay focused on what's in front of you to do. Sometimes we can get control of our minds by simply putting things in place around us, creating physical order around us. Making our beds, doing the dishes, vacuuming the floor, brushing our teeth. By restoring order in our external environments, the mind can become more relaxed and trusting.

We can also focus on elevating our mood. By engaging in practices that make us feel lighter, happier, or better about ourselves we will be more resourceful when it comes to handling the stressors in our lives. What actions can you take to elevate your mood? Does going for a walk or exercising improve your mood? What views or attitudes would help you step out of your comfort zone and in the direction of your dreams? How could you speak to yourself in an empowering way? What thoughts, affirmations or self-talk could improve how you feel about yourself? What could you tell yourself to help you connect with your confidence? Are there certain songs that make you feel good? Does dancing get you out of worry and into a more relaxed physical state? What can help you create a state of positive expectancy?

10. Employ your contingency plans as needed. If challenges come up, refer to your contingency plans. Life is not always agreeable, and neither are people. Know that there will be moments of disappointment or setbacks. Learn to be flexible, rise up to meet life's challenges, and find your center. These are valuable coping strategies.

11. Assess and celebrate. Review the steps you've taken. Acknowledge yourself for facing your fears. Celebrate any success you've had moving forward on your dreams and moving through your fears.

12. Stay focused on where you want to go. See yourself succeeding. Envision yourself accomplishing and living your heart's desires. See yourself getting through whatever circumstances have created the fear. Envision yourself confidently resolving situations. See yourself succeeding at whatever endeavor you are engaged in. If that's too much of a stretch, imagine yourself successfully engaged in the process of creating or doing whatever you're going after. For example, if your dream is to be happily married, imagine yourself going on dates and being at ease with yourself and the other person. If your dream is to be a screenwriter, imagine yourself enjoying the process of writing. If your dream is to own a yoga studio, imagine yourself leading yoga classes to a full room of people happily stretched out on their yoga mats at the end of a yoga session. If your goal is to be successful at public speaking, imagine your friends sitting around you at a dinner party totally engrossed in the story you're telling.

As you move toward your fear and engage in behaviors you're afraid of, you will expand your comfort zone. One of the reasons to expand your comfort zone is that you'll learn that many of the things you fear the most don't happen. The things that do happen you will face, step by step. You'll be able to address your concerns, find solutions, and ultimately move through your fears. No matter where your journey takes you, keep your mind engaged in and focused on the direction of your dreams.

Failing Forward

Even if you fail—often our worst fear—remember to fail forward. *Failing forward* means that even if you're not getting the outcome you desire, you are still moving toward the realization of your dreams when you're following the guidance of your heart. You are still learning and investing in your growth and mastery.

No one wants to fail. However, if you never try to succeed, you'll never know what's possible. Harvey Milk, the first openly gay politician to run for office, ran for San Francisco city supervisor three times before finally winning. Each time he ran, his number of supporters grew. Each time, he empowered other LGBT people to come out of the closet. He failed forward.

The same was true with the marriage equality movement. There were multiple losses, but with every loss, as people continued to share their personal stories, the movement gained more and more supporters for marriage equality. Finally, the poll numbers showed that the majority of Americans supported equal marriage rights for same-sex couples and a federal law was enacted.

This is what failing forward looks like.

My client Andy was afraid of putting himself back out in the dating world after a breakup. His failing forward took the form of asking women out on dates and learning how to create meaningful connections with them. His first attempts were met with rejection. Eventually, he became comfortable asking women out and facing his fear of rejection. He built his confidence and soon met a woman who became his girlfriend.

Good Fear

We all have automatic physical reactions to threats to our wellbeing. In moments of perceived danger, the fight, flight, or freeze aspect of our nervous systems is activated. When we see a snake on a hiking trail our hearts beat rapidly, our bodies fill with adrenaline, and we become hyperalert. We take action to make sure we are not bitten. This is good fear.

Good fear can keep us safe and alive, helping us identify threats in our environments. Good fear can get us to run from an attacker or get out of the way of a speeding car.

Bad Fear

Unfortunately, human societies are filled with amorphous threats, and some of our reactions to them are counterproductive. For example, fear can get us to engage in behaviors that are unhealthy and selfish. Overeating or using substances, such as alcohol or marijuana, to numb our feelings is one way our response to fear can harm us. Fear can get us to push people away or to hoard money or belongings because we are afraid we won't have enough. Fear can create a sense of competition and greediness and we can become restrictive emotionally and financially not engaging openly with the people around us.

Fear can be used to manipulate us. Many of our fears are not our own. They are conditioned in us by social, religious, and corporate agendas. You may already be aware that mainstream society is focused on keeping you obsessed with safety and security. For example, car commercials, insurance commercials, and cold and flu commercials are all designed to get you to buy products by creating a sense of fear in you. This can be true with the news and political agendas as well.

Fear can create pain in the absence of any real source of pain. Fear can cause us to project danger on to something that cannot harm us. This is where the acronym False

Evidence Appearing Real is apropos. Remember the snake situation I was discussing earlier? We see a snake. Our hearts race. We sweat. We look for our escape. But what if we discover that the snake is just a twisted stick? We just expended energy getting worked up about an illusion.

These responses are meant to be protective and come from the part of our brain that's wired for survival. You can see this in veterans with PTSD. They hear fireworks and drop and cover to protect themselves from bombs lodged in their body's memory. These bombs went off while they were in combat, and no longer exist.

When we have an interaction with another person that feels similar to something from our past that hurt us, it can trigger a physical fear response. It's an emotional projection that creates a physiological fear response like when we see a twisted piece of wood and assume that it's a snake.

When we prejudge situations that seem familiar to us, assuming they will be exactly the same, it can cause us to close down, become defensive, or push to protect ourselves. Motivational speaker Lisa Nichols refers to this as "punishing your next because of your ex."[1]

Fear can keep us from taking action. Fear can have a paralyzing effect on us, keeping us from pursuing our dreams, making changes in our lives, and even leaving bad situations because we fear the unknown or that we could find ourselves in an even worse situation. Fear can keep us from taking advantage of opportunities for growth and change. Fear can keep us focused on mere survival when we have the ability to thrive and expand.

Where is fear stopping you from taking action? What in your life makes you afraid? What are your responses to fear? Is fear triggering you to engage in unhealthy ways of reacting or coping? In what ways do you feel manipulated to feel fear? Are you aware of any fear projections you have? Have you ever found yourself overreacting with a new person because something in the interaction with them felt similar to a situation from your past that hurt you?

Expanding Your Comfort Zone

As you begin to confront the things you're afraid of, and you realize you don't die from your fears—whether they involve public speaking, flying, or traveling outside your country—you'll begin to expand your comfort zone. As your comfort zone expands, you'll feel more competent and consequently confident—and *confidence* is a good synonym for *faith*.

Every time you act in alignment with an insight from your deeper self, and each time you take an action that you might initially be anxious about, you begin to create a new self-concept. You begin to view yourself differently and to feel more comfortable taking actions that were previously outside of your comfort zone.

My client Carl was terrified of bridges. Every time he had to cross the Bay Bridge from Oakland to San Francisco, he panicked. His heart raced. He broke out in a cold sweat. He gripped the steering wheel so hard his knuckles turned white. Needless to say, Carl's life was seriously limited because he avoided attending events that involved bridge crossings. This might have been fine in some cities, but in the Bay Area, crossing at least one bridge is a necessity to get to almost any destination.

I worked with Carl to help him conquer his fear of bridges. By using baby steps and a combination of psychological and coaching methods, we shifted his mental and physical state. I guided his focus, his self-talk, and his body language. I also took Carl through the process of systematic desensitization, an approach proven to address phobias.

Carl and I began our work together over a cup of coffee at a Starbucks located near the edge of a drawbridge known as the High Street Bridge in Alameda, California. For the record, his cup was decaf. The High Street Bridge crosses over 296 feet of the Oakland Estuary. Once I had worked with Carl to tap into his courage both mentally and physically, we walked across the bridge together. I coached him every step of the way, keeping him focused on his goal.

Carl had to fight his instinctive urge to retreat back to solid ground. He had to keep his eyes focused on the other side of the bridge, rather than on the water below. He had to endure the shakiness in his body and the racing of his heart. He braved on and soon found himself safely on the other side of the bridge. This was when something began to shift in him. He had a new sense of confidence. But we didn't stop there. We crossed again and again for the next hour. Carl began to notice that he was less shaky each time. He began to see himself differently. Carl began to see himself as a man who could cross bridges.

Our second meeting took place at the Park Street Bridge in Alameda. This bridge spans 372 feet of the Oakland Estuary and is an open-grate bridge, making the water below visible to those crossing it. The open-grate feature presented some new challenges for Carl. I worked with Carl to find his courage and engage the proper mindset and physicality to tackle this new hurdle. This time as we crossed, Carl began running across the Park Street Bridge trying to get the crossing over as quickly as possible. Even so, he saw that he was able to do it. And do it again he did. Before long, Carl and I were walking back and forth across the bridge and he had embodied the mental mindset and physical presence of someone who could easily cross a 372-foot open-grate bridge. Crossing bridges of this length and construction had become congruent with how he saw himself.

Carl and I continued working together for several months and our victory lap was meeting up at the Golden Gate Bridge, a mile-long suspension bridge that crosses over the Pacific Ocean and San Francisco Bay and connects the San Francisco Peninsula with Marin County. While we didn't have time to walk the full length of the bridge and back, we did walk to the center of the bridge. Once there, we stopped and snapped a photo. In it, Carl is enthusiastically smiling with his arm around me. I was so proud of him.

A few months later, some rather random scenarios that Carl had feared could happen actually occurred on the Bay Bridge that connects Oakland and San Francisco. I had previously minimized Carl's fears, thinking them irrational, until a steel crossbeam and two steel tie rods snapped on the San Francisco span during the evening commute. This bridge malfunction occurred on October 27, 2009, and closed the bridge for a week. Then approximately two weeks later on November 9, 2009, a semi-truck went over the barrier in the area known as the S-curve section of the Bay Bridge, killing the driver. This was a new span that had only opened two months previously in September 2009.

Nevertheless, Carl's progress remained and he happily relocated to San Francisco with a new courage for crossing bridges. It wasn't that he went from being a pessimist to being an optimist. He saw himself as a realist who had conquered his bridge phobia. The shocking events that occurred on the bridge during that time period, were a part of Carl's realism.

Creating New Neural Pathways

Every time we do something new, we begin to create new neural pathways. A neural pathway is a connection between brain neurons that allows electrical signals to be sent from one part of the brain to another. Creating new neural pathways hardwires these new behaviors into our brains, making them more congruent with how we perceive ourselves.

When we are learning a new language, our brain makes new neural pathways. For example, let's say you learn that *gelato* is the Italian word for ice cream. There will be a connection between the word *gelato* and where you store the phrase *ice cream* in your memory. When you hear the word *gelato* you will make new connections within your auditory cortex. When you conjure up a picture of ice cream in your mind and name it *gelato,* you will create a neural pathway within your visual cortex.

It may take some time to override existing neural pathways to create new ones. For example, a client of mine from the United Kingdom shared with me how he adjusted to driving on the right side of the road in the United States. Initially, he found himself turning into the wrong lane and only when he saw oncoming traffic did he realize his mistake. What felt wrong to him was the right way to drive in the United States.

If you begin to make changes in your life and they evoke fear or feel wrong at first, don't automatically decide that what you are doing is wrong for you. Imagine if my British client had told himself, "Since I keep turning onto the wrong side of the road, this must be the right thing." It would have led him down a destructive road and a tragic ending.

Additionally, the fear you feel that something is wrong may be an automatic response created by the programming from your family and culture. Don't go back to the old way or bury your head back in the sand of your old routine. Like learning to drive on the other side of the street, making changes in your life may take some time getting used to. It's going to feel strange at first, but soon your brain will adjust to the new changes you're making.

We will discuss gratitude and appreciation in the next chapter.

INVITATION

Choose an action you want to take in your life or something you want to change. Assess the level of risk you're willing to invest and then begin the twelve steps of moving through fear presented earlier in the chapter.

CHAPTER NINE

Become Magnetic to Good

"Feeling gratitude and not expressing it is like wrapping a present and not giving it."
—William Arthur Ward

As a therapist, I began seeing Melanie, a trained actress, for depression and anxiety. Having moved to Hollywood from Miami three years previously to begin her acting career, she was considering giving up on her dream completely and moving back home. Given that she hadn't booked a commercial in months and had yet to be called back for any roles in movies or television, her attitude was understandable. The few experimental films by students she'd appeared in were nothing like the career she dreamed of.

During our work together, I suggested she begin keeping a gratitude journal. Perhaps you first heard of keeping a gratitude from Oprah or self-help books like *The Secret*. In her book *What I Know for Sure,* Oprah shares how she kept a gratitude journal in which she wrote down five things she was grateful for every night for ten years. She recalls that she felt qualitatively happier during those years. She says that the act of connecting with her gratitude helped her delight in life's goodness in a way that she lost track of when she stopped keeping a gratitude journal. "You radiate and generate more goodness for yourself when you're aware of all you have and not focusing on your have-nots."[1]

And you don't have to take Oprah's word for it. While some people may view the practice of keeping a gratitude journal as a silly pop culture self-help practice, psychologists have conducted studies that show that people who write down what they are grateful for report feeling happier and more excited about their lives.

One study conducted by psychologists Robert Emmons, Ph.D., at the University of California, Davis, and Michael E. McCullough, Ph.D., at the University of Miami, found that people who write down what they are grateful for are more likely to exercise, complain less about health issues, and have fewer visits to the doctor.[2] This study also found that people who write down what they are grateful for feel happier and more optimistic about their lives.

Another study at Brigham Young University found that people who express gratitude for their partners feel better about their partners and are more comfortable expressing concerns about their relationships, so those issues can be addressed.[3] In his book *Thanks! How Practicing Gratitude Can Make You Happier,* Emmons presents the numerous health and wellness benefits, like this one, that come with engaging in a regular gratitude practice.

My reason for suggesting that Melanie keep a journal was to activate an inner radiance that would activate an experience some people refer to as the *law of attraction.* You've no doubt heard of this metaphysical law, the principle that like attracts like, which is often misunderstood to mean that if you just think something consistently and strongly enough, you'll magically cause it to materialize. Of course, that's not the case. We must do more than think about what we want to attract into our lives. We must become the kinds of people who attract the situations we want to appear in our lives by being available to them, showing up in our fullness, and going after what's important to us.

In a nutshell, when we have an attitude of gratitude, we're more likely to draw to us and be drawn to the kinds of opportunities and experiences that evoke our appreciation.

To help Melanie get started down this track, we spent the first ten minutes of our sessions focused on what was going great in her life. Before long she was finding that the more she practiced gratitude, the more she had to appreciate.

As time went on, Melanie began meeting more people in the Industry, as the film and TV business is called in Los Angeles. She found herself being invited to all kinds of social gatherings that could help her career—and not the kind you might envision, where young actresses are taken advantage of by producers and directors with nefarious agendas.

What was happening?

Melanie's newfound appreciation for life had generated an enthusiasm that made her irresistible. She was so fun to be with that she was literally drawing successful actors, directors, and producers into her social circle. Naturally, her new friends began advocating for her. Even though she had no agent, these major producers were seeking parts for her. Within a year of almost throwing in the towel, acting opportunities, auditions, and callbacks were a regular part of her weekly schedule.

Appreciation Is Magnetic

Appreciation is defined as a "feeling or expression of admiration, approval, or gratitude" and as an "increase in value."[4] When we appreciate something, it appreciates in value to us. The act of appreciation and connecting with feelings of gratitude can make us magnetic to circumstances and experiences that will give rise to more expressions of gratefulness. I believe that appreciation creates a positive state of resonance within us.

Resonance is when our energy is amplified by the energy we meet in another person. If you strike a tuning fork next to a piano, the piano string of the same key will begin to vibrate. When we share the same enthusiasms and respond similarly to experiences, our heart "strings" sing a happy note. We connect and feel both akin and uplifted.

Metaphysicians believe that a positive resonance increases our vibrational frequency. The higher the frequency, the lighter we feel. The happier. The more energized. By contrast, a lower vibrational frequency is associated with emotional states like depression, fear, and anger. Resonance is when like attracts like.

Gratitude shifts the vibrational state within us, raising it up. Since like attracts like, gratitude leads us to be a vibrational match to greater goodness. At the very least, the act of engaging in active appreciation increases our tendency to view the world in a more favorable way, rather than focusing on what's wrong which is more frequently our go to state. Psychological researchers have identified a phenomenon they call *negativity bias,* whereby people tend to place more value on the negative aspects of an experience than on the positive aspects.[5,6] Negativity bias may also contribute to *negativity dominance,* where we label an event negatively, even when it has positive aspects. Because of this tendency to remember the negative more than the positive aspects of an experience the positive aspects of experience don't remain with us as long as the negative aspects linger.[7]

In my estimation, the positive internal state created from connecting with our gratitude is sufficient justification to engage in a practice of conscious appreciation. This brings joy to your essential self. When you are feeling grateful, loving, and appreciative, you are speaking the heart's love language. Your heart loves it when you delight over the small things—the smile on a child's face, the smell of a good cup of coffee, the way the leaves on a tree dance in the wind, the crisp morning air, the feel of the sun on your skin.

Cultivate an Attitude of Gratitude

Why wait for something to make us happy when we can engage in intentional practices that make us feel good immediately?

It's no secret that one of the ways to get yourself into a positive frame of mind is to ask questions that pull you into a state of gratitude. We can engage in "courageous appreciation," where we allow ourselves to fall unapologetically in love with life.

You'll know this is happening when you want to take a moment to smell the flowers, catch yourself spontaneously taking deep breaths, and begin saying hello and making eye contact with strangers. You'll also find yourself feeling happy for no apparent reason. For me this also includes telling the people in my life, from close friends and family members, to my dry cleaner, colleagues, and so on, how much I appreciate them. I just enjoy letting people know how much they mean to me.

To evoke gratitude, try asking yourself questions like: "What am I grateful for today?" "What do I appreciate about my: life, job, body, sweetheart/spouse, home, family, friends, community, self?" "What do I love about my life, job, body, sweetheart/spouse, home, family, friends, community, self?" and "Where is love present in my life?"

I used this same strategy with a client who was a professional artist. In the first ten minutes of our sessions, I insisted he focus on his "wins" for the week. Wins are things that are going well. Only after we discussed what was going well did we discuss what wasn't. From this process, I noticed he had a tendency to omit the big successes in his life, dwelling instead on which career goal hadn't happened yet. By learning to focus on what was going well and really amplifying his gratitude, he was able to connect with his success rather than just driving by it.

There was also a powerful spinoff from this. By taking the time to slow down and feel positive emotions associated with what he had accomplished, like being happy about the accolades he was receiving, his confidence as an artist grew. He felt more congruent when calling himself an artist. As his confidence grew, he was offered more opportunities to show his work, which of course meant that he was making more money. It even got to the place where he was able to let go of the part-time commercial art job he had clung to for financial security, even though he didn't enjoy it and it left him emotionally depleted. In fact, the first year after he quit the part-time job, he was commissioned to paint a work that brought him the equivalent of a third of the annual pay he received from that job. By connecting to his gratitude on a regular basis, he was more inspired, more magnetic to opportunities, and more available to pursue his passion as an artist. He was also able to exercise greater control of his life and make choices that empowered him. Empowerment was a byproduct of his gratitude practice.

I need to point out that the confidence my client developed wasn't the sort that comes from boosting the ego, which ultimately has no real substance. Rather, it was confidence rooted in his trusting, believing heart—a confidence drawn out by the accolades he was receiving, not based on them. It was his true self that gave him his confidence, not a borrowed confidence based on the validation of others.

A fulfilling life is as close as tapping into appreciation, slowing down, and connecting with yourself by being with your own company, finding your own rhythm, being fully in the moment, and not waiting for the world to give you a reason to smile.

In the next chapter, we will explore how to slow down and nurture yourself, which is an integral part of taking back your life and the next step in the hearticulation process.

INVITATION

In your journal or a notebook, at least once a week write down eight things for which you are grateful. Include the big things and the little things that are often taken for granted. For example, you might say: "I am grateful for my eyesight, my hearing, my fingers and toes, my ability to speak, my sense of taste and smell." You want to really anchor yourself in how lucky you are and how good life is. You want to create a deep sense of gratitude because gratitude opens your heart and when your heart is open you can connect more deeply with the true you! When you connect with the true you—your essence—it's easier to know what's really important to you. From this place, you will be able to listen to the voice of your higher self speaking to you! That's the best you!

If you want to take it a step further, every day you can engage in what I call the Grateful Eight. Write down eight things you for which you are grateful. This will keep you connected to what's good in your life. You could turn it into a social media post and invite others to write what they're grateful for too. Use the hashtag #GR8FUL.

CHAPTER TEN

Nurture Your Authentic Self

"To love oneself is the beginning of a lifelong romance."
—Oscar Wilde

D o you use loving, encouraging language when you speak to yourself? Or do you put yourself down? For instance, do you stand in front of the hall mirror and say, "I look fat" or "I'm ugly"?

What kinds of things did you hear growing up? Were you told you were lovable by your parents or caretakers? Did they tell you that you were smart, pretty, handsome?

When I worked with incarcerated women, I was shocked to discover that many of them never heard the words "I love you" from their mother or father when they were children, which fueled their belief they were unlovable. They didn't realize that this failure was likely because their parents themselves were never told they were loved either.

Even more insidious was the fact they internalized a belief that they were unlovable because they also heard statements like "You're stupid. You're fat. You're ugly. You're just like [insert some disliked relative here]. You're no good. You're going to end up in prison."

And guess where they ended up?

Many of my Native American clients' parents were taken from their parents at a young age and raised in Indian boarding schools by well-meaning clergy whose aim was to "kill the Indian and save the man." Their parents, and even some of my older Native American clients, were shamed and beaten at these boarding schools for "speaking Indian" or practicing traditional Native American spirituality. Far from being nurtured as children and developing healthy self-esteem, these scarred and wounded boys and girls were taught to hate themselves. Then when they grew up and had children of their own, they didn't know how to nurture them.

I found a lack of nurturing by parents and an inability to nurture themselves was common among my clients whose families had been involved in war, revolution, or extreme trauma, and also when their parents or caretakers were drug or alcohol addicted. These clients were likely to have been physically neglected and abused as children, so that they also had no concept of how to nurture themselves. Instead, they learned how to numb and escape by indulging in alcohol, using drugs, smoking, overeating, and other activities that briefly can make us feel better, but ultimately harm us. They confused addiction behaviors with self-nurturing. Additionally, clients who grew up with strict authoritarian parents who demanded perfection of them, which is not uncommon in rigidly religious households or military families, often lacked the experience of being nurtured and thus didn't know how to nurture themselves. Even when we do receive love and nurturance from our parents or other family members, there's a whole world out there that isn't always as encouraging. We've all heard mean things from our peers. Some of us were bullied for being different and verbally abused and called names.

Also, when we began dating and engaging in romantic relationships, rejections or breakups likely impacted how we felt about ourselves. By allowing ourselves to love someone so deeply that their opinion of us mattered, we exposed ourselves to comments that in many cases crushed us. It's one thing for the neighborhood bully to tell us we're ugly, fat, or stupid, but when it's our lover or spouse who's pointing out our physical or personality flaws—and who keeps finding new ones we weren't already insecure about—these experiences can add up, making it feel difficult, if not impossible, to love ourselves.

We are so used to picking ourselves apart. Since we know our own flaws intimately, this is easy. Every blemish, every mistake, every shortcoming lurks somewhere in the back of our minds, ready to draw our attention to it when we're having a bad day—and even when things are going well. We can so easily believe we are unacceptable. After we've run through our own list of reasons why we are unworthy of our own love, we're likely to focus on the things other people have said or done, or failed to say or do, to cause us to feel unlovable.

If you find yourself beginning to put yourself down by calling yourself derogatory names, for instance, step in front of a mirror, stand there intently looking at yourself, and quietly listen to all the things you are saying about yourself. As you observe the negative, critical, and derogatory things your head tells you about yourself, should you become sufficiently still you'll notice a deeper reality in the background against which all this negativity is taking place. The experience I'm talking about is akin to sitting in a movie theater watching something unpleasant unfold on the screen and feeling appalled by what's being portrayed. Often, we get so engrossed in a movie that we forget it's a movie. But when something shocking occurs, we suddenly step back mentally and become aware that it is, in fact, just a movie and not reality. Well, you can do this same thing by observing your thoughts.

When you hear your head beginning to talk to you, notice what it's saying, and at the same time notice the effect this has on you. If you pay attention, you'll see that there is a deeper you that doesn't feel this way and that is shocked at what your head is telling you about yourself. This is your very *being*.

Your being knows the truth. It knows you are able to make wise choices. It knows that you are loved. It undercuts all the negative self-talk of the head, which is shallow by comparison.

Loving Self-Talk

A strategy to help us stay connected to our essence is loving self-talk. Loving self-talk cannot get you connected to your core self if you haven't done the work to strip away the layers of falsehood and excavate your essence. Just like Michelangelo did when he was sculpting his famous statue of David, you must chip away all that is not your essence. Affirmations can help you uncover and connect to the beauty of who you are and spark your inner flame.

An affirmation is a positive assertion expressing something we would like to be true that begins with the words *I am*. Loving self-talk like this is a gateway to get us moving in the right direction. Affirmations help us to be mindful of our words, adhering to that which Buddhism refers to as *right speech*.

The value of an affirmation isn't to talk you into believing something that isn't true of yourself, but to help you become aware of what is true. You can remind yourself when the gremlins come out that "I am a good person, I am loved and lovable." Refrain from negative self-talk and if you catch yourself engaged in it, employ affirmations.

Here's how to use affirmations appropriately. Affirmations are more effective when they are spoken out loud on a daily basis. For example, you might stand in front of mirror, look into your eyes, and greet yourself with, "Hey, beautiful being," "You're looking good today," or "I love you." Maybe *Saturday Night Live*'s Stuart Smalley comes to mind. Go ahead and laugh.

It helps to embody the affirmation. Hence, if your affirmation is "I am confident," it would be best to say this while you're sitting up straight or standing up, shoulders back, chest out. Although affirmations cannot make your wishes magically materialize, they can be used to lift your mood and refocus your mind when used in combination with other psychological and spiritual practices. I will speak more about this in Chapter 17, "Keep the Faith and Follow the Flow."

Beyond saying affirmations is the practice of self-affirmation whereby we connect with and affirm our core values. In her book *Presence,* social psychologist Amy Cuddy, Ph.D., shares that connecting with our core values boosts our self-worth. She describes self-affirmation as the "practice of clarifying your story to yourself, allowing yourself to trust that who you are will come through naturally in what you say or do."[2] Cuddy suggests that "your boldest self emerges through the experience of having full access to your values, traits, and strengths."[3]

This is great to know for those of us who already have a sense of our self or our values and value who we already are. However, what do you do if you're not there yet?

One of the biggest blocks to our happiness and success in life is our inability to fully love and accept ourselves. You've heard the cliché: Before you can love someone else, you have to love yourself. It's really true.

Take a moment to reflect. When you're feeling good about yourself, what do you love and appreciate about yourself? What do other people say they appreciate about you? If you're in a downward spiral it may take some stretching to get there. It's worth it to dig deep and come up with some specific things you and others appreciate about yourself. Once you've established some of those beneficial aspects about the authentic you, begin affirming them.

This practice will have a positive impact on your life. In 2013, an international team of psychologists found that self-affirmation can increase the problem-solving performance of people under chronic stress and buffer them against the negative effects of stress.[4]

The point of self-affirmation isn't to get into a mental struggle against the negative thoughts and cultural messages playing in your head. This isn't an attempt to make something true, and it isn't about making something happen. Rather, it's to help you become aware of your already peaceful, joyous, loving center. It's ultimately of little use to affirm, "Hey, beautiful being," "You're looking good today," or "I love you," unless you know in your heart what a simply lovely, lovable, and loving person you actually are.

If you choose to post affirmations around your house, let them be reminders of who you are, not attempts to "get there." You are already there. This is why I have an affirmation posted by my desk that reads, "I am the leader I've been waiting for." Another favorite affirmation I created and say to myself is, "I am a beautiful, unique contribution to the human tapestry."

Spiritual teacher Eckhart Tolle makes an insightful point in one of his recorded lectures in which he discusses affirmations, commenting that when you truly embrace your truth, you don't need an affirmation to reassure yourself of it. For instance, he says, billionaire businessman Bill Gates doesn't need to have an affirmation on his bathroom mirror to help convince him that he's wealthy.

The springboard to self-love is to awaken to who we really are and to the love that's our true nature. This differs fundamentally from the tactic of trying to argue ourselves into loving ourselves. However, we need to do more than just stay in our head, constantly reassuring ourselves of our worth, telling ourselves, "I love you!" Because if we do, then no sooner do we affirm our love for ourselves than the voice in the head contradicts us. It's a forever battle. When we can actually feel in our heart the love we've been denying ourselves and others, this love will bypass all the contradictory self-talk of the head.

Ultimately, feeling true love for ourselves isn't something we can talk ourselves into—and neither can we talk anyone else into it. We must reclaim our essence and feel the surety and perfection of our core being—unique and magnificent, something each of us must come to experience by and for ourselves on the journey of the courageous heart. This is what life is trying to teach us.

Self-love involves being our own best friends and chief nurturers. It means being there for ourselves to pick up the pieces when life throws us curveballs. We need to pick ourselves up, kiss our own booboos, and soothe ourselves. We need to be able to speak lovingly to ourselves when life gets tough and not let our inner critic run wild blaming, shaming, and pointing fingers at ourselves while bringing up past hurts and saying, "See I told you so!" Self-love means we learn how to accept ourselves with all our flaws and foibles. Real self-love means forgiving ourselves for our mistakes and learning how not to make those same mistakes again.

Self-love differs radically from narcissism. Self-love is the practice of caring for ourselves and finding ourselves worthy of our own kindness and respect. In narcissism, we measure ourselves as lesser or better than others from a core sense of being inadequate and not having healthy attachments with a primary caregiver as an infant. Narcissism is a serious attachment disturbance whereby we are constantly seeking out affirmation from others to prove our worth. Self-love is knowing that everyone is special and that no one is special and accepting ourselves for who we are and who we aren't. Self-love is caring for our own needs for affirmation first, rather than using others to fill an unceasing, childlike need for admiration that seems to exist with persons with narcissistic traits.

Self-love also allows us to love our neighbors as ourselves. When we are lovingly connected to our authentic selves, a deeper awareness emerges of the connection of all life. It's another example of *Mitakuya oyasin*—we are all related. In Mayan culture, people greet one another with the phrase *"In lak'ech,"* which means "I am another yourself." The response is *"Ala k'in,"* meaning, "And you are another me."

Many more cultures and spiritual traditions hold our oneness as a fundamental teaching. In Christian teaching, we find the statement "Love your neighbor as yourself." Buddhism teaches "There are no others." To harken back to

Shakespeare, when we are true to ourselves, we cannot be untrue to anyone else, which really means that once we love ourselves and our true nature, it will be easy to love our beloved fellow travelers on the journey, warts and all.[5]

Once we touch this deep place inside us, this beautiful essence, and we remember our own radiance, how do we keep ourselves from hiding it under a bushel? And how do we keep from losing ourselves again?

Nurture Yourself

Many of us have been taught to put other's needs before ours. Perhaps we witnessed the selflessness of a parent or we grew up with religious teachings that admonished selfishness and advocated selflessness, even martyrdom. Self-love is demonstrated in the practice of self-care and self-nurturance.

Basic self-nurturance involves making sure that you're exercising regularly, drinking adequate amounts of water daily, eating nutritiously, going to the dentist regularly, getting checkups, taking your medicine if you have a chronic health condition, refraining from damaging habits like smoking, overeating, and substance abuse, and getting eight hours of sleep every night. That is basic self-care. Many people struggle with it.

Basic self-care is critical to keeping yourself up and running. However, doing the basics is not enough. If you want to live a full life, take self-nurturing to the next level.

Connect with your essence. Make time for daily meditation, reading books that uplift you, writing in your journal, going on dates with yourself where you do things you love, and taking down time to rest. When you are living a heart-based life, you are more sensitive to energy around you which can cause stress. Regular meditation and downtime will help you to deal more effectively with life's stressors.

Engage in self-care and relaxation practices. Make time for meditation. Sit quietly and breathe deeply. Take a relaxing bath at the end of the day. Schedule monthly massages or facials. Engaging in other self-care practices that reduce your stress level will help you to stay grounded and relaxed. Don't wait until you're frazzled. Build regular advanced self-care practices into your weekly schedule.

Be proactive about your health. Practice proactive health measures that bolster your health and keep you strong and vibrant rather than simply reacting to illness. For example, don't wait to get sick. Instead, work regularly with an acupuncturist or holistic practitioner for structural support and to bolster your immune system.

Invest in your personal growth and mental health. Basic self-care is responding to a crisis, such as a major loss, divorce, depression, by seeking support. Advanced self-care is investing in your mental health and personal growth on an ongoing basis. Through personal development courses, regular coaching, therapy, workshops, or other forms of personal growth work, you can continuously work on healing old wounds, learning healthier communication skills, correcting thinking errors, and growing your self-confidence and ability to love and accept yourself. Self-development workshops, therapy, and coaching can help you understand your motivations and reactions to situations and people and can empower you to make more mindful decisions and take more thoughtful actions.

INVITATION

Create a list of ten things that are specifically nurturing to you, such as getting a massage, reading in bed, taking a warm bath, sipping tea, and writing in your journal. You may want to keep this list somewhere accessible so that when you're having a bad day you can quickly refer to the list and plan to do one or more of the ten things on your list. You can also download a Self-Care Assessment on my website: FollowYourCourageousHeart.com.

Once you're engaged in gratitude and self-nurturing practices, you're ready to become integrated. Embracing your wholeness is the next step in the hearticulation process.

CHAPTER ELEVEN

Embrace Your Wholeness

"Individuality is only possible if it unfolds from wholeness."
—David Bohm

I met Amanda while working in a federal women's prison in California. Amanda had dissociative identity disorder (aka multiple personality disorder). During our work together, I witnessed some thirty-three different personalities, each one an aspect of her original self that had fragmented during horrifyingly traumatic, severe incidents of childhood emotional, physical, and sexual abuse.

One personality, Carrie Ann, carried Amanda's artistic skills, which she had been punished for expressing as a child. Another personality, Anthony, was a protector. He was gay. He was protective of the other personalities because Amanda hadn't been able to stop the abuse she and her siblings experienced at the hands of her severely disturbed parents. This personality was created gay when Amanda was anally raped by her stepfather. A third personality, Monica, was allowed to express anger and rage.

As a child, when Amanda expressed her anger at being physically and sexually abused, the abuse became even more violent. Monica carried all the childhood rage and would explode any time Amanda experienced frustration.

Amanda herself had no memory of the incidents in which she manifested these personalities. She would lose hours and sometimes days. I met some of these personalities during her "blackouts." Naturally, they precipitated multiple problems in her life. I helped Amanda integrate the parts of herself that had split off. It was healing for her to reclaim these fragmented sides of herself, enabling them to communicate with one another and work together.

While dissociative identity disorder is rare, all of us have disowned certain aspects of ourselves and need to integrate them back into our lives so we can move forward as whole beings. We often don't realize we've split off those parts of ourselves that weren't appreciated by our parents or peers both in childhood and adulthood. Many of us leave parts of ourselves behind on our paths at different times for various reasons, including wanting to be liked and fear of rejection. We abandon parts of ourselves to please others and fit in.

Sometimes our abandonment of ourselves is in little things, like not listening to certain radio stations anymore when you're with people who don't like that kind of music, or not talking about certain subjects when you are with people who don't want to talk about politics or spiritual beliefs. Sometimes it's no longer doing the things that make your heart sing, like no longer dancing because your partner doesn't like to go out.

In romantic relationships, we often call this losing ourselves. Losing yourself feels bad.

In order to get back into your power and live from your authentic center, you need to reclaim your lost parts. To lead a fully self-expressed, heart-based life requires integrating these neglected or disconnected "personalities."

One of my private coaching clients, Deanna, loved nature and really wanted to travel the world. Unfortunately, since Deanna was the only daughter born of immigrant parents from Latin America she felt it was her duty to remain in her family home caring for her elderly parents. While we worked together, it occurred to her she had stopped buying plants and going on hikes because anything related to nature brought up sadness that she wasn't living her purpose or even on purpose.

Deanna had stopped valuing herself and her heart's desires, and perhaps consequently, others in her life also failed to value her. This was especially true in her work, where she found herself taking on more than her fair share of duties. Deanna had been at her job for five years yet hadn't received a single raise. Every time she tried to bring this up to her supervisor, he would cut her off or change the subject. We worked on how she could bring herself back to herself and begin living a life that honored her values.

One of Deanna's coaching goals was to speak up for herself and finally ask for a promotion. She decided that if she was not given a promotion she would seek employment elsewhere, someplace where her efforts would be recognized and rewarded. Our coaching together prepared her to take action that showed she valued herself and her heart's desires. She asked for the promotion, her boss declined, and she stuck to her principles. Deanna made the choice to leave her old job and found a new job with opportunities for growth and promotion.

When she completed her coaching sessions with me, Deanna was working in a new position where she felt valued and was confident that she would never again lose sight of her own self-worth. Deanna felt that this was the most important outcome. She had learned to set the bar for how she was willing to be treated.

No matter how positive our background, we must still each go through the process of losing sight of ourselves for a time, only later beginning to awaken to who we have always intrinsically been—something that often happens as we approach midlife.

The process is aptly described by T. S. Elliot in the poem "Little Gidding":

We shall not cease from exploration
And the end of all our exploring
Will be to arrive where we started
And know the place for the first time.

Perhaps we've spent years trying to become something different from our essential nature. We've worked hard to add letters and degrees to our name to prop ourselves up. We've focused on adding numbers to our net worth to create some sense of self-worth. These are straw men that must be burned down so we can see the essence of our nature, our core being, which we expressed in our childhood before we started hiding and shapeshifting to gain love and attention. When we strip away from ourselves all the layers of dust and grit from the journey of our lives, our soul shines through and we delight in our true being, rather than trying to love some false self whom we've never been.

I've watched adults in my group counseling sessions and in one-on-one sessions reclaim their true natures, and it's powerful. They remind themselves of the things that mattered to them, like nature, music, art, creativity, freedom, self-expression, being a geek that loves taking things apart to see how they work, dancing with fairies in the garden, singing passionately at the top of their lungs, making up stories, and performing for the sheer joy of being able to play and imagine worlds beyond this one.

This reclamation is way bigger than reclaiming your "inner child."

This is about reclaiming your *essence*.

Reclamation is about sitting with yourself and letting your true self lead the way. It's about owning your essence and moving forward in life from this center. You can't allow any supposed need for social approval cause you to abandon yourself. Don't let any imagined need to be "nice" stop you from being authentic. Any need to cater to the needs of others is masochistic if it causes you to sublimate either your essence or your own needs in order to care for others. Service is not servitude. Don't let anyone take your light. If you find you have, take it back. Your essence is yours. It is the core of your being. You don't need anyone's permission to express your essence. Embrace your wholeness and shine!

In the next chapter, you will learn how to acknowledge previous wounds without keeping yourself stuck in the past.

INVITATION

Look deeply at your life. Where are you giving yourself away? Are there any people you find yourself giving up your power to, or abandoning yourself to be with? This can be a very hard inquiry. We often ignore red flags. We don't want to see where we've given more than we should. We justify why we've given up so much of the things that make us happy to make others happy. Once you identify your danger zones, make a pact with yourself and enroll a good friend, to help you take back your time, energy, and resources and restore your wholeness.

CHAPTER TWELVE

Let It Go and Move On

*"Forgive us our trespasses as we forgive those
who forgive those*
who trespass against us."
—*The Lord's Prayer*

O ne of the biggest obstacles to experiencing ourselves as the loving person we are is our inability to forgive ourselves. We feel guilt and shame for mistakes we've made. We beat ourselves up for situations we handled less skillfully than we might have wished. We incriminate ourselves for the people we've hurt—whether accidentally, unconsciously, or intentionally. To fully love yourself and unleash your courageous heart, you must be able to forgive yourself.

We also struggle with forgiving others. Perhaps you've been betrayed. Maybe someone hurt you, stole from you, lied to you, or was unfaithful to you. It may feel hard to forgive in such a situation. However, not forgiving will rob you of your energy and keep you stuck in the past. You won't feel good or hopeful about life.

Not everything we approach openheartedly is going to work out as we expect. Not everyone we open our hearts to is going to treat us as we wish. Most of us will experience disappointment in love, and likely we'll disappoint others. However, if we can trust that everything we go through is an opportunity to learn—an opportunity to know ourselves as the loving people we are, and hence to be compassionate to others—forgiving their mistakes and accepting their decisions as we would want them to do with us—then our loads will be lighter, and our paths will be easier to walk.

Voices of Forgiveness

Forgiving is courageous. To unleash your courageous heart and secure the items you put on your courageous heart list, forgiveness must be a way of life for you. Most spiritual leaders throughout time have spoken of the power and importance of forgiveness.

For example, the Jewish mystics known as Kabbalists teach that if we want to be forgiven for our mistakes, we must forgive others of theirs.[1] If we are unforgiving, it creates a barrier between ourselves and the Divine. In the New Testament of the Christian Bible, Jesus is quoted as saying, "Father, forgive them; for they know not what they do."[2]

Spiritual and civil rights leaders have also placed a premium on forgiveness. Gandhi encouraged the Indian people to forgive the British Colonists. In the 1950s and 1960s, before his murder, Reverend Martin Luther King, Jr., called on African Americans to forgive the pain and suffering inflicted on them by white segregationists. He saw forgiveness as a catalyst for healing and creating the atmosphere for a fresh start. Emphasizing that forgiveness is a prerequisite of love, he described it not as an occasional act but as a permanent attitude. Without the ability to forgive, we cannot love. The former president of South Africa Nelson Mandela, who led his nation in healing after Apartheid, emphasized the importance of letting go of grudges, explaining, "Resentment is like drinking poison and then hoping it will kill your enemies."[3]

The exiled Dalai Lama of Tibet has stated that compassion is one of the most important spiritual attributes and one of the most important qualities for human connection.[4] He says that when we are unwilling to forgive, we cut ourselves off from the ability to develop compassion and thus are unable to move forward on our spiritual paths. Until we can remove our sense of anger, frustration, desire for revenge, and feeling like we are a victim, we will suffer and won't know peace. But if we cultivate patience and tolerance, we will be able to let go of negative feelings, so that forgiveness then comes easily.[5]

Contemporary spiritual teachers also emphasize the power of forgiveness to help with everything from inner peace to prosperity.

Edwene Gains, author of *The Four Spiritual Laws of Prosperity,* identifies forgiveness as part of her third law of prosperity. Describing forgiveness as *emotional housecleaning,* she says that when we forgive ourselves and others, we "make room for the good we desire."[6]

Author Marianne Williamson, in her book *A Return to Love,* also talks about the power of forgiving ourselves and others. She believes that "forgiveness is the key to inner peace" because when we forgive "our thoughts are transformed from fear to love."[7] She also sees forgiveness as a full-time job. She says we must practice *selective remembering* focusing only on the love and letting the rest go.

Williamson says we are challenged to forgive because our ego is like a hungry dog that looks for every scrap of evidence to find fault with ourselves and others. She comments, "The ego always emphasizes what someone (us or someone else) has done wrong."[8]

In contrast to the ego, the soul knows that *only love is real,* and that to forgive is to turn toward love, rather than loathing, blaming, or judging ourselves or others. How are we to deal with the pain of being hurt? Williamson suggests that sometimes the hurt we've experienced actually allows us to become more compassionate and loving. She writes, "Sometimes it takes a knife that emotionally pierces our heart, to pierce the walls that lie in front of it."[9]

Radical Forgiveness

Colin C. Tipping, author of *Radical Forgiveness* and *Radical Self-Forgiveness*, amplifies Marianne Williamson's statement that it can take a knife to pierce our heart. He states that the "forgiveness process involves realizing our spiritual being created this situation for our spiritual benefit."[10] According to Tipping, radical forgiveness is the process of seeing there was a "divine purpose in what happened to us."[11]

Tipping suggests that a bonus in viewing the events that hurt us as opportunities for spiritual growth is that they can help move us out of *victim consciousness,* where we identify and define ourselves by painful experiences. He advises us to reframe our memories of such situations from "what the person did to me, to what the person did for me."[12] Now it becomes a way to advance ourselves spiritually.

When we view anything that has occurred within the context of our higher spiritual self, we shift the energy from negative to positive.

Tipping suggests we use the following affirmation:
I release the need to blame myself and to be right and I am willing to see the perfection in what is just the way it is. I am willing to see that my mission or 'soul contract' included having experiences like this—for whatever reason.[13]

Everything we do that requires forgiveness is an opportunity to evolve spiritually. The trick is to integrate lessons learned from experiences that call for us to forgive ourselves or others into the bigger picture of the journey of following our courageous hearts. When we view these experiences through this larger framework, it begs the questions: "How am I a different person because of this experience? What options are available to me that weren't before? What choices should I make now?"

Even if you don't believe in a higher power or a higher spiritual purpose, would you be willing to consider that whatever wound you sustained through being wronged by another has taught you something or brought forth something in you: perhaps a previously undiscovered strength or some new knowledge that ultimately benefited you or made you a better, wiser, stronger person?

To open our courageous hearts and live from our authentic centers requires rubbing shoulders with each other, which involves hurting each other's feelings, not appreciating each other, and even at times distancing each other—all the behaviors we fall prey to as humans sharing the planet together. If we continue following our truths, we eventually move beneath the veneer of what each of us seems to be and discover the Divine.

Whereas holding on to blaming others or ourselves for wrongdoing keeps us stuck in the past and anchored to negative emotions, forgiveness can bring us happiness and peace. It takes courage to offer forgiveness to others when their thoughtless or selfish actions have affected us, as well as to stop beating ourselves up for poor choices we may have made.

Keep in mind that you have chosen to take the journey to open your heart so you can experience greater feelings of happiness and peace. Exonerating yourself and others is essential to this opening. To be able to offer the balm of forgiveness to yourself and others is to stay connected to your life force. If you believe in a higher power, letting go of grudges and resentments will keep you open to Source itself.

The next step in the hearticulation process is releasing perfection.

INVITATION

Make a list of the people you are still feeling hurt by. Then, holding one at a time in mind, go through these questions. What did the person do to me? How am I a different person because of this experience? What is it costing me to hold on to my unforgiveness toward them? Am I willing to take my energy back from them? Can I allow myself to forgive them even though I wish they hadn't done what they did?

CHAPTER THIRTEEN

Release Perfectionism

"Perfection is shallow, unreal, and fatally uninteresting."
—Anne Lamott

Perfectionism is the notion that something must be an exact way otherwise it is deplorable. That anything less than "correct" cannot be tolerated or allowed. This attitude creates a tendency for us to view anything less than 100 percent as unworthy of recognition. Perfectionism is a striving for being flawless in one, many or all areas of our lives. From the "perfect" score on a test, to having the "perfect body," the "perfect relationship," the "perfect child," or being the "perfect parent." The medical definition of *perfectionism* is a "disposition to regard anything short of perfection as unacceptable; *especially*: the setting of unrealistically demanding goals accompanied by a disposition to regard failure to achieve them as unacceptable and a sign of personal worthlessness."[1]

Perfectionism sets us up for failure and self-loathing. Perfectionism is associated with depression, eating disorders, anxiety, low self-worth, and even suicide.[2] Being flawless, perfect, or being someone who never makes mistakes is not something we should be striving for.

Rather than striving for some unattainable standard of perfection, it's crucial to allow ourselves to be human and lovable, faults and all. By loving ourselves with our imperfections, we develop greater compassion and a stronger connection to our shared humanity. If we did something we now regret, perhaps whatever we did provided us with an opportunity to open our hearts to other people's struggles and challenges. Part of forgiving ourselves is to be able to accept that we aren't going to do everything to the standard of perfection often held up to us.

Priscilla, a recently graduated social worker I coached, was plagued by perfectionism. Not only did Priscilla feel she could never do enough to help others, her head was forever telling her that she could do "better." No matter how hard she worked, how many people she helped, her head wouldn't let her off the hook. The consequence was that she felt exhausted to the point of burnout. Priscilla longed for rest and for a chance to be creative again, but she was caught in the neverending cycle of responding to others' needs.

To help her see the perfectionism that was driving her, holding her hostage, I had Priscilla imagine a Zen garden, then imagine a beautiful scene in pristine nature. Both are exquisite. However, the Zen garden requires constant care to keep it beautiful, whereas nature just needs to be left alone. Nature contains bugs. It also has dead and decaying leaves and branches. Yet who would argue that it isn't perfect as it is? Mother Earth doesn't need improving on. The

Zen garden, on the other hand, is only beautiful because of the tremendous work that went into creating it and the constant tending required to maintain it.

Perfection is the head speaking to you. The head judging you, finding you and others lacking in some way, if not incompetent. The head will keep pushing you to do more, urging you to try to achieve some impossible standard from a place of guilt, fueled by the fear of "not enough."

Parents are often plagued by perfectionism. Parents in today's culture with the powerful influence of the "hungry ghost," worry that they're not doing enough for their children. This seems to be more common with mothers. You can see this played out, especially around their children's birthday parties. It used to be enough to celebrate a child's birthday by having a gathering with pizza and cake, or taking the kids bowling or to the roller-skating rink with friends. Nowadays kids' birthday parties are catered. Video arcades on wheels come to their house. Jumpers are rented and clowns and magicians are employed. Kids are taken on expensive adventures with their friends like going to amusement parks or laser tag venues. Birthday extravaganzas. Events with big price tags, plus lavish presents. Divorced parents sometimes try to outdo each other or make up for the other parent's absence or for their own feelings of guilt and failure about being divorced. Perfectionism drives them away from the authentic generosity of the heart and into the ego mind's never-enoughness and lack consciousness.

The heart does not play the game of perfectionism. It doesn't keep score. The heart accepts and loves. The heart will move you to action, not from trying to fill the hungry ghost, but from a place of joy. It will stir your creativity. When the heart is in the driver's seat you will feel a contentment with yourself, accompanied by a feeling of peace and wholeness.

Your heart requires no upkeep. It is pure just as it is. Your head, on the other hand, needs constant weeding. Your mind requires constant pruning to keep it functional.

When Priscilla could look at herself in this way, something melted in her, and her heart began to open. She described feeling a warm sensation in her chest, which spread throughout her body. She began to see the unnatural standards she was holding herself to, and how she was good enough just as she was. "I feel like the fog is clearing," Priscilla told me as she made a commitment not to be driven by the perfectionism of her head but to listen to her heart.

Maybe you stumbled your way through the past year. Perhaps a lot of things happened that baffled you. Perceptions, misperceptions, people's statements, things that happened or didn't happen—you have no clue how to even begin to make sense of some of it.

Yet the authentic journey of the courageous heart asks us to be in this moment, now, and to be content to live with not knowing, confusion, and bewilderment. This is what faith is—being fully present each step of the way despite unanswered questions and imperfection.

In Lewis Carroll's *Alice in Wonderland*, the Duchess advises Alice to just be what she seems to be. Well, that's my advice to you. Through all of life's moments added together, you will live the life you need to live. You will increasingly express the person you already are in your essence. Far from the Divine being some perfect "other" that's completely separate from you and your life as you experience it, it's through all that's transpiring in your life that the Divine is pressing you to know yourself in ways truer to your essence.

In each moment, we can only ever be as we seem to be, even though this may be far from any fantasies we hold in our heads of who we're supposed to be. The mistakes, the perceived inadequacies, the confusion, the things we've said and regretted, the things not said, the wavering—all of these are an essential part of carving a meaningful path through life.

The whole of it, whether joyous or painful, is part and parcel of the process of becoming true to yourself, true to your purpose, true to your uniqueness.

The Divine isn't experienced only in what goes right by our criteria, but in the foibles and ambiguities of everyday life, with our ambivalence, our two-facedness, our hypocrisy, our deceit and self-deceit. Something magnificent lies beneath the surface of everyday existence, seeking to break through. But it's only as we traverse the mire of everyday living and relating to each other that it gets a chance to breathe and come alive. There is no seed germination in the pristine, the pure, the perfect. Seeds germinate in the muck and must break through the darkness and dirt to emerge a seedling.

Without some time in the trenches, the journey of self-discovery never quite kicks into gear. Locked in the prison of our own self-imagined purity, we never plant the proverbial seed of our essence into the mud and muck needed to give ourselves a chance to grow. What may seem to be so imperfect at any given moment ends up being the fertile soil that allows us to germinate and grow the fullest expression of ourselves. It's in the seeming imperfections, failures, and disappointments that our path unfolds. So, bless the mess. It is in the mess, not an imagined perfection, where the Divine is found.

Mythologist Joseph Campbell saw this, which is why he says, in *The Hero with a Thousand Faces:* "The two worlds, the Divine and the human . . . are actually one."[3] There's a deeper dimension to all of us. The deeper will emerge, if we neither delude ourselves nor run from the fray.

In the next chapter, we will explore how you may improve the quality of your relationships.

INVITATION

Take a moment and allow yourself to accept and embrace your perceived failures and faults, all that you judge to be defects and deficiencies, as a perfect part of your perfect path. Accept and embrace them. Now, let these perceived shortcomings open your heart and bring forth your compassion for your own and others' humanity.

CHAPTER FOURTEEN

Improve the Quality of Your Relationships

"The quality of your life is in direct proportion to the quality of your relationships."
—Anthony Robbins

D o you have close friends you can talk to when you get stressed out or need support? Do you take the time to invest in your friendships, connecting with people besides your immediate family? Are the people you hang out with emotionally available or self-absorbed and consequently unreliable? Will your friends only go so deep?

It's important that you have people in your life you can call at 1:00 a.m. if you need to. These are people who love you unconditionally, who see the good in you, and who are also not afraid to call you out when you start to call yourself down. If you don't have good friends in your life, it's time for you to make new friends. You need to find people who are emotionally mature and have a willingness to be with you in the messiness of life.

What kind of friend are you? Have you been too self-absorbed? Are you a fair-weather friend? If this is the case, then you need to become a better friend to others. Do you need to show up for someone who may be going through a meltdown, rather than always being too busy when people reach out for support? Is it time for you to say yes to helping someone move?

Or maybe it's the other way around and you are being the rescuer. Are you one who takes care of everyone else and doesn't let anyone support you?

Having balanced relationships is an important component of living an authentic life.

Being able to give is just as important as being able to receive. In fact, they are two sides of the same coin. Ernest Chu, author of *Soul Currency,* a book about financial prosperity, says that people who are unable to receive block the flow of circulation, the giving and receiving of money. He makes the case that if you are mostly a giver who isn't open to receiving, your means of giving will eventually dry up and you will no longer be able to give. Just as we exhale and give our breath, we must inhale and receive a breath, or we will suffocate.

When we aren't open to receive, we deny the other person a chance to be the giver. Sometimes allowing others to give to us brings up feelings of unworthiness or vulnerability. This is good because we need to address any feelings of unworthiness. We need to face our fear of not being in control, facing up to whatever keeps us from being flexible. It's a matter of unclogging those arteries that block the circulation of give and take.

By no means is this easy. If you have a strong urge to be "in control" because you suffered a trauma, grew up in an alcoholic or dysfunctional family, or because you had a problem with parents or partners seeking to control you, this will challenge you. I still struggle with judging myself when I feel vulnerable and in need of emotional support from friends. However, letting go of the need to be in control all the time and allowing ourselves to receive is part of the journey of the courageous heart and a pathway to greater authenticity. Don't see yourself as burdening people.

Real friends can support us in being true to ourselves and so it's important to have solid ties with people we can turn to when our spirits are down. Fair-weather friends on the other hand can take from us and turn on us. If you want to live an authentic life you want to cultivate supportive relationships with other authentic people. In Chapter 15, "Engage the Power of Synergy," I will discuss how to connect with kindred spirits and make connections that support you in living a life you love. Here, we'll explore how to create and maintain meaningful relationships and what to do when you find your relationships thwarting your authentic self-expression.

People with Your Best Interests at Heart

Steven Pressfield, author of *Turning Pro,* talks about how people in your life change when you commit yourself to your dreams. He says that those who are "still fleeing from their own fears will now try to sabotage us." He adds, "At the same time, new people will appear in our lives. They will be people who are facing their own fears and who are conquering them. These people will become our new friends."[1]

As you embark on a path of personal evolution, you'll find that the world has plenty of naysayers, and it isn't possible to simply avoid them. They are everywhere. Naysayers are simply people who are inexperienced when it comes to following their hearts, which means they have a hard time seeing the positive in situations. They've been conditioned by their families or by fear to see and anticipate the negative. For them, it's about survival and being in control. Keep in mind that naysayers aren't born that way. Under the right circumstances, they can become the openhearted, positive thinkers and talkers of the kind you want in your tribe.

You may find that some of the naysayers in your world will want what you have and will come to you for guidance. The key is to focus on moving your life forward, not on seeking such people out in the hope of bringing about change. When you are ready and they are ready, let them come to you. There's no need to save them from themselves—that's their job. Your job is to focus on *you*. Once you follow your personal truth, people may shake out of your life like leaves on a tree in autumn. Don't see it as a bad thing. Recognize that it's a natural part of the season of the soul's growth and evolution. Knowing which people are rooted in your life versus likely to blow away with the breeze is an important stabilizing factor.

This is why it's crucial to surround yourself with people who support you in being true to yourself, especially when society urges you to sell out, or at least stay quiet, "for your own good." True friends don't tell us how to live, something only *we* can know. They can share their love and concern with us, however unless we are going to take an action that would physically harm ourselves or others, we are the ones who know best what decisions to make for our lives.

When my marriage ended, some people I considered close friends told me I should stay in my marriage and put the marriage equality movement above my own happiness. Ironically, it was my heterosexual friends who saw my breakup as simply entering into another facet of marriage equality already familiar to many of them—divorce.

Beyond the difficult and painful ending of my marriage, I got to see who my real friends were. If I'd been honest with myself I would've recognized the chaff from the wheat. True friends don't love you because of what you do for them or for the image of who they think you are or who they want you to be. True friends don't need you to be a certain way. They will love the you that is continually growing and unfolding, not a sculpture frozen in time.

Often your best friendships will be with people who follow their hearts, have had to make tough choices, and have gone through difficult changes in their own lives. They are willing to be open and vulnerable.

When you are connected with other authentic people, they help you stay true to yourself, encouraging you as you rebuild your life should circumstances or other people bring you down. Allowing others to support you is an honorable, even sacred, gift. Yes, my friend, you are blessing others by allowing them to support you.

What about People Who Don't Have Your Interests at Heart?

If you find some of the people in your life don't seem to have your best interests at heart, what should you do?

Sometimes one of the most effective action is doing nothing at all. You may find that as you begin to move in the direction of your heart's calling, those who don't really have your best interests at heart will simply stop calling you or inviting you to events. In that case, your task is to soothe any hurt feelings that may arise about being out of the circle.

There may be other people in your life who continue to call you for favors or because you benefit them in other ways, but the relationship is more parasitic than mutual. If this is the case, you are being given an opportunity to say no. When you say no to things that aren't important, it frees you up to say yes to things that are.

Now, to be clear, I believe it's important to help your friends out and to support your community by volunteering your time and talents. However, it's also important that there's a mutuality in your relationships. Friendship is either a two-way street or it's not friendship. You want to know your friends are going to be there for you as you are for them, which means they need to support you in being true to yourself. In such a situation, honesty is the best policy. If you find people in your life who don't support you, speak honestly with them and give them the opportunity to respond. If this doesn't work, you may wish to stop accepting their invitations and simply say "no" or "I'm busy." If you're busy enough times, they'll likely stop asking you.

What about Family Members Who Don't Have Your Best Interests at Heart?

What do you do if the people who don't have your best interests at heart are your family members? As with the other people in your life, I recommend talking to them and expressing your concerns. Share with them how you feel. Perhaps they don't understand what you are doing or why you're doing it. Perhaps they're afraid for you, frightened of where your path is taking you.

It's important to make a distinction between family members who are unsupportive in a neutral way, versus family members who are antagonistic and perhaps even malevolent. Yes, it's nice when family cheer you on and enthusiastically support you. However, it's not your family's job to be your 24/7 cheerleader. A neutral "Do what you want with your life" response isn't damaging. On the other hand, in the case of family members who are openly hostile to your choices, or who inflict mental, verbal, or physical harm on you, share as little about your heart's desires as possible. You might also need to minimize, if not eliminate, your contact with them.

What If Your Spouse or Partner Doesn't Have Your Best Interest at Heart?

The biggest concern people usually have in following their hearts and being authentic is the fear of losing an intimate relationship with a partner or spouse. I'm often asked what do I do if my partner or spouse doesn't support me?

First, you need to ask yourself is it true that your partner or spouse doesn't have your best interests at heart? There are lots of reasons your spouse or lover might not want you to follow your dreams. The most obvious is that your path might take you away from them, which could lead to the end of your relationship. That's bound to be threatening to anyone. In such a situation, how should you move forward?

The first thing to do is to assess whether this is a relationship you want to remain in. If it isn't, you may be unconsciously communicating something to your partner that feels like rejection, which triggers an antagonistic response toward your calling. I recommend that you go to therapy or get some other form of support to help you and your partner end the relationship with integrity.

If you want to remain in your relationship and work together to explore your partner's fears or concerns about the changes you're making in your life ask your partner or spouse if they are willing to go to counseling or seek support. If they are, you can explore the changes that are taking place together in a safe, supportive environment. You will each need support to navigate the changes ahead. Hopefully each of you can follow your own heart's calling, while simultaneously supporting one another in being true to yourselves and learn to manage any fear or jealousy that arises.

If your partner is not willing to go to counseling, you can still get help. A good counselor functions as a kind of mirror or sounding board, whereby you share your thoughts and feelings with them and they reflect back to you what they are hearing and seeing in you. Counselors can offer suggestions and options, but no counselor should ever tell you what to do. The point isn't for someone else to direct your course, but simply to help you see through the fog of your mental and emotional confusion so that you can follow your own internal compass.

Growing Together or Growing Apart

Sometimes we expect our spouse or partner to love everything we love and want them to do everything we want to do. It's fine for couples to enjoy different activities, different challenges, and different callings, and in a healthy relationship we each accept our differences. You can't demand your spouse join you on every activity and you can't demand they constantly validate you. An important aspect of maturing is to self-validate. Sure, it's nice when a person who is important to us affirms us, but it needs to be a bonus, not a requirement.

In his books *Seat of the Soul* and *Spiritual Partnership*, spiritual teacher Gary Zukav makes a distinction between marriage and spiritual partnership. He defines marriage as a legal partnership in which the goal of the two people is to assist in physical survival. A spiritual partnership, on the other hand, is a relationship in which two people are together for spiritual growth, what he calls the "conscious evolution of the soul."[2] Zukav writes in *Spiritual Partnership*: "Potential spiritual partners recognize the commit-ment, courage, compassion, and conscious communications and actions of one another. They naturally strive to support one another in creating authentic power and to receive the support of one another in creating authentic power."[3] He suggests that for people on the spiritual path, a marriage without spiritual partnership will become stagnant and dissolve.

If your mate doesn't want to grow together, it may mean that at some point the relationship ends. Be willing to surrender to that and let yourself grow and shine your light regardless of their decisions. Your authentic soul path awaits you.

INVITATION

Take an inventory of the friends in your life. Do you have people in your life with whom you can be your authentic self? People you can call on in case of an emotional or other emergency? Do you have friends who would bring you soup if you were sick? If you don't have at least one of these kinds of good friends in your life, then it's time for you to make new friends. You need to find people who are emotionally mature and have a willingness to be with you in the messiness of life. It is equally important to take a look at yourself. When was the last time you helped a friend in need? When was the last time you took someone soup, gave them a ride to the airport, sat and listened to their fears and encouraged their dreams? It's never too late to become a better friend.

In the next chapter, we will explore how to up level your inner circle and engage the power of synergistic relationships.

CHAPTER FIFTEEN

Engage the Power of Synergy

"You are the average of the five people you
spend the most time with."
—Jim Rohn

I n twelve-step programs, they say that if you want to make lasting change in your life, you need to change your *playground*, your *playmates*, and your *playthings*. The people you are surrounded by influence your behavior. Malcolm Gladwell asserts in his book *The Tipping Point*, that environment is one of the strongest influences in our lives. He calls it the "power of context."[1] Gladwell maintains that human behavior is so strongly influenced by environment that it can play an even bigger role in our lives than our family upbringing. Environment, more than family upbringing, influences the clothing we wear, whether or not we smoke cigarettes, go to college, attempt suicide, engage in high-risk sexual behavior, or engage in other prosocial or antisocial behavior.

As Stanford social psychologist Philip G. Zimbardo, Ph.D., showed in his famous 1971 study, the Stanford Prison Experiment, the power of context can even cause normal people to engage in cruel and unusual behavior toward others.[2] In this study, Zimbardo converted a basement into a mock prison cellblock and divided students into prisoners and guards. The prisoners were "mock arrested" by the Palo Alto police department. The "guards" became aggressive and abused their power and the "prisoners" became depressed and despondent. The experiment, which was planned for two weeks, was discontinued after six days because of the sadism of the "guards" and the damage it was doing to the psychological and physical well-being of the "prisoners."

The power of context played a huge role in Cupcake Brown's life. Cupcake—yes, that's her real name—was once a homeless, gang-affiliated, crack-addicted prostitute. Today she's a New York Times best-selling author and attorney for one of the nation's top law firms.

After reading about Cupcake in the local paper, I invited her to come speak to a group of female inmates in my Second Chances program at the federal prison. When I met Cupcake, she had just graduated from law school. She hadn't yet passed the bar exam or written her book, *A Piece of Cake.*

Cupcake shared how important it was to leave her old crowd behind so she could create a new life for herself. She knew she couldn't remain in her old crowd and live an authentic life that honored her dreams. Many of her old friends felt threatened by her aspirations and wanted to keep her partying. She said she gave her friends a choice, they could join her on the road to recovery or get out of her way.[3] It was black and white for her. Her friends could either get clean and sober, or they were out of her life.

The old story about crabs in a barrel illustrates why we must have the right people around us if we want to be true to ourselves. As I've heard it, apparently if you have a bunch of crabs in a barrel and one of the crabs begins to crawl out, the other crabs will pull it back into the barrel. If they could speak, they might say, "Who do you think you are? You think you're better than the rest of us?"

If you are surrounded by people like those crabs in the barrel, they won't want you stepping out of the barrel and into your power. For this reason, it's important to surround yourself with brave souls who are willing to live life outside of the proverbial barrel.

Cupcake talked about a time when no one in her new environment would talk to her because they believed someone from her background didn't belong in law school. Luckily, she found supportive people in twelve-step meetings. She shared that with the encouragement of her sponsor and fellow twelve-step members she developed the confidence and courage to go after her dreams. Cupcake's story underscores my point that if you want to make lasting change and live a life that honors the true you, you need a supportive environment and supportive people.

The Power of Synergy

By connecting with people who are also choosing to make changes and follow their dreams, especially those who are on a similar path of transformation, you can tap into the power of synergy. *Synergy* is the "interaction of elements that when combined produce a total effect that is greater than the sum of the individual elements contributions."[4] Synergy is about teamwork, it's working together to create bigger and better results than if we just did something alone.

In 1999, I contacted the Anthony Robbins Foundation, which is committed to helping underserved populations. I wanted to get Tony Robbin's permission to teach his curriculum at the federal women's prison I worked at. Becky Robbins, Tony's first wife, even made a trip to the prison to speak with the female inmates in one of my groups. She inspired them to follow their dreams and not let limiting beliefs (an important tenet of Tony's work), stop them.

We all have let limiting beliefs, negative mental programming, hide our true essence. This negative mental mindset was even more pronounced with my incarcerated clients. They had terrible self-esteem, were addicted to drugs and alcohol, and chain smoked. Most of them were significantly overweight and rarely exercised. They didn't think they could do much other than commit crime, and thought of themselves as victims—for good reason, given that more than 50 percent of them had experienced horrible abuse as children and adults.

My goal was to create a tribe of women who were breaking through limiting beliefs, inspiring one another. Prisons have their own tribes. They're called *gangs*. Prison gangs are usually divided by race or ethnic group, share a distrust of "The Man" (meaning, traditional, usually white, male authority figures), and are focused on the distribution of contraband.

I wanted to empower these women to make positive, healthy changes in their lives. True empowerment always consists of awakening a person's awareness to the innate power of their essential being. This empowerment isn't something I or even Tony Robbins could confer on them. What we could do was evoke within them their own inherent power.

What resulted was a powerful circle of women who were supporting one another in actualizing their fitness, education, and personal goals. The synergy generated by these women as they worked together to transform their health was phenomenal. I watched women collectively shed hundreds of pounds, quit smoking, and become vegetarian. They supported one another in giving up soda and candy bars, while also increasing their water consumption. Some went from never having exercised in their life to working out five times a week.

One woman, Carol, decided to teach herself how to lead spin classes on the archaic stationary bicycles in the prison's gym. She began offering spinning to her classmates and other inmates at 6:00 a.m. These women were transforming before my very eyes.

The tribe grew as other inmates noticed the changes in my graduates. The changes were so noticeable, and these inmates were so positive, that I began receiving comments from the staff, who were stunned by what they saw in the women. The ripple of positivity even caught the warden's attention.

This experiment allowed me to witness the incredible power of the collective heart, even in dark places like prison.

Creating Synergy

Surrounding yourself with people on the path of transformation will help you overcome challenges and make the kinds of changes you desire. If you want to transform your life in a particular way, you will fare far better if you create synergy by connecting with likeminded or similarly goal-focused people.

For example, if you want to get in shape and lose weight, you'll want to connect with people who are committed to a healthy lifestyle. You can join a gym, take up yoga, enroll in Zumba, Bollywood, or Hip-Hop classes. You can even sign up for a half-marathon training program and make some new friends. Choose an activity that you believe you will enjoy.

If you want to start a business, spend time with people who are also starting their own businesses, have successful businesses of their own, or who at least believe in your ability to start and run a successful business. You'll want to hang out with solopreneurs and entrepreneurs. You can join a meet up, a chamber of commerce meeting, a professional networking group, or a business mastermind.

If you want to be a successful actor, artist, writer, or singer, you'll need to connect with those who are doing similar things. Sign up for an acting, painting, writing, or music class. Just remember to keep those courageous-heart qualities in the front of your mind, you don't need to add any crabs in your barrel.

Additionally, to live your authentic life, you want people in your life who share a similar desire to follow their heart and be fully self-expressed. People who are on the path of courageous authenticity with you. They are fellow believers in being true to ourselves. They are positive thinkers, dreamers, and optimists—people who support your dreams and are doing the kinds of things you want to do.

You don't need to feel isolated, even if you live in a location where these kinds of tribe members are hard to meet with in person. You can find online communities that are brimming with loving, positive people who are more than willing to support you in following your courageous heart. For example, you can join my Courageous Heart online community and get the support you're seeking (see Resources).

You'll also want to surround yourself with individuals who believe in your talents. This will be especially important when you go through periods of self-doubt, which will inevitably happen, especially as you begin taking steps to follow your courageous heart. This isn't about propping up a flagging sense of yourself by getting a transfusion of selfhood from others. You can never build an authentic sense of self by leaning on others. If you rely on others to prop you up, you will eventually find yourself falling apart. Rather, you want people in your life who help you to discover your *own* unique center. People who reflect back to you, aspects of your own authentic self, people who remind you of the fact that everything you need, you can find *only* in yourself.

Building Your Heart-Based Tribe

Because the collective is so powerful, it's important to be selective when choosing who you invite into your inner circle.

When you start to build your heart-based tribe, look for people who believe that *internal* factors determine a person's success, not external factors. Find people who believe that it's not what happens to you in life that matters most, but what your response is. These are people who have what psychologists call an *internal locus of control*. In contrast, people who have an *external* locus of control believe that what their life becomes is the result of what happens *to* them.

No matter what life sends your way, you can do far better than simply trying to survive or get by. When your mindset is one of merely enduring, you turn yourself into a victim of circumstances. The person with an internal locus of control realizes that their thoughts, beliefs, attitudes, and actions can shape their circumstances, giving them a powerful say in how situations unfold.

Studies have shown—and my own experience as a counselor bears out—that people who believe they have some personal agency in determining the course of their lives are happier and more self-confident than those who believe that life simply happens to them and there's little they can do about it. For this reason, you want to surround yourself with people who know that the economy, the job market, or other external factors don't determine a person's ultimate success and happiness.

Success, like happiness, is an *inside* job.

If you find yourself in a blue moment and starting in on your Debbie Downer routine, don't beat yourself up. Just recognize that discontent (anti-bliss) is rearing its ugly head. With this realization in mind, consciously make an attitude adjustment as quickly as you can to get yourself back on track. It can be as simple as finding something to feel appreciative of, something good about your life. Make the choice to go with your emerging authentic being, not those ingrained negative neural patterns that haven't yet been disconnected and replaced.

If you've been used to just allowing life to happen to you and feeling sorry for yourself as a result, you need to know that such a trait isn't in any sense a given like your height, eye color, or skin tone. You can change the way you respond to each and every situation that arises. If you choose to feel that life is victimizing you—if your thinking revolves around how dreadful your circumstances are— you'll invite more of the same. You'll feel victimized by people, the place you work or live, and your circumstances. On the other hand, an attitude of gratitude, along with a mindset that elicits your trust in yourself, calls forth the empowerment that comes from knowing we live in a friendly universe.

I am a huge admirer of Nelson Mandela, who could have so easily claimed victim status. He clearly got a raw deal in life. However, he's someone who fully embodied an internal locus of control. Instead of becoming bitter and resentful during his twenty-seven years as a political prisoner of apartheid in South Africa, he prepared to lead his country. He mastered the art of forgiveness and compassion, so that when he was released, he had the personal fortitude, the leadership skills, and the public respect to be elected president.

I'm sure you realize that it's good for your health to be around positive talkers and thinkers, as well as to be a positive thinker and talker yourself, I'm not referring to "bootstrapism" (picking yourself up by your bootstraps), which is just another way of bolstering the ego. I'm referring to the positive thinking and talking that results from allowing our deliriously joyous center to govern every aspect of our lives.

Studies have found that people who are more positive live longer because they are less likely to have cardiovascular problems.[5] Even when they do have health issues, positive thinkers are more likely to exercise and stay positive in the face of these medical challenges. Some studies have even found that being positive is a protective factor against illness in general.

When I refer to positive people, I don't simply have in mind people who see the good in everything in a Pollyannaish kind of way, or even people who can always find something to be grateful for, fine qualities though these may be. I'm talking about people who choose to live authentically by following their heart and expressing their gifts. It's important that the people closest to you, who you spend the most time with, are growing, learning new things, and taking positive risks in their lives.

You also want people in your tribe who are willing to stretch themselves. Such individuals have a big vision, and are willing to risk looking foolish, or even failing, in service of their larger dream of living wholeheartedly. Such people view seeming disappointments as opportunities that lead to inevitable success. These people embrace change and don't need you to stay static so they can feel secure. They can help you stay focused on the good stuff, so you remember that even setbacks that look like failures can be reframed as *setups* intended to catapult us forward.

Of course, you'll need to engage in practices that help you act in these ways and embody these qualities. As you do, you will attract more of these kinds of people into your life.

Your Invisible Tribe

Your synergistic tribe doesn't have to be made up of only people you know personally either. You can create synergy by connecting with leaders, celebrities, and public figures, living or deceased, who inspire you through their books, films, and speeches. You can even connect with them the old-fashioned virtual way: in your mind, through visualizations.

In the classic book *Think and Grow Rich,* Napoleon Hill mentions that, every night, he connected with a group of powerful men in his mind, including people like Abraham Lincoln, Thomas Edison, and Henry Ford. Hill referred to them as his *invisible counselors.* Over a period of several years, before going to sleep at night, he "held an imaginary council meeting" with a group of nine such men. During this meeting, he called on each to impart the knowledge he wished to receive from him. "I had a very definite purpose in indulging my imagination through these nightly meetings," he explains. "My purpose was to rebuild my character so it would represent a composite of the characters of my imaginary counselors."[6] For example, Hill wished to receive a "keen sense of justice" from Lincoln, "marvelous patience" from Darwin, and a "spirit of faith" from Edison, and so on.[7]

As I pointed out earlier, so again here, it isn't a matter of copying someone else, trying to be them. Rather, we allow them to evoke in us the wonderful traits of justice, patience, and faith, and so on. These are all already part of our inherent makeup and simply need to be drawn out.

Part of living a life that honors your authentic self is not to be stopped by the conventional idea of reality. As a popular bumper sticker reads: Question Reality.

Open yourself up to the idea that what you think of as reality isn't always as real as it seems. For example, it was once considered a reality that the world was flat, that slavery was acceptable, and that shock therapy would help gay people become straight. Just because we believed these things to be true didn't make it so. We must question reality, our own and society's, so we can lead lives that reflect the deeper truth of who we came here to be—lives that honor our dreams and desires.

Just as we create much of our reality with our thoughts and beliefs, we can create new versions of reality that more accurately serve our needs and aspirations.

In the next section, we will explore how to navigate the twists and turns on the path of authentic living. Your focus will be to stay open to the unfolding.

INVITATION

Take a look at the five people with whom you spend the most time. How do they impact you? Does their presence in your life create more joy, more possibility? Does their presence in your life make you a better person? Are the top five people in your life adding to your overall wellbeing or taking away from it? Are you satisfied with this? If not, who would you like to spend more time with?

What kinds of people would you like to include in your inner circle? What changes do you need to make? Do you need to schedule some time with these folks? Do you need to join a group? What actions can you take if the person is not immediately accessible to you? How can you virtually connect with people who are going to help you create the kind of synergy that would support you in being fully self-expressed? Your best yet to be?

Conversely, are there people it would behoove you to spend less time with? People who drain your energy? People with whom you find yourself engaging in negative mental states or behaviors? What could you do to remedy this?

Part Three

Stay Open to the Unfolding

CHAPTER SIXTEEN

Expect Twists and Turns

*"Our job, as souls on this mortal journey, is to shift the
seat of our identity from the lower realm to the
upper, from the ego to the Self."*
—Steven Pressfield

You never know where your inner compass will take you. Alvaro certainly couldn't have imagined where following his heart would lead him. Alvaro grew up the child of migrant workers and was the first in his family to graduate from college. His parents had toiled in the fields to provide for him. After completing his undergraduate degree, Alvaro cashed in on an opportunity to travel to London on a work visa program for graduating students. This three-month trip turned into three years, and he found himself traveling all around Europe.

About a year and half into his European journey, Alvaro began feeling guilty for not returning to the United States to start his career. He felt he owed it to his family to accomplish the middle-class American dream they wanted for him and for which they had sacrificed. Yet, he couldn't bring himself to buy a return ticket. He felt that there must be a reason he didn't want to go back—that there must be something he was supposed to do, even though he didn't know what it was.

Alvaro got a work permit in Ireland, then bought a Eurail pass and began traveling from country to country. The opportunity arose for him to go to Granada, Spain, where he took a job at a hostel. When some of his coworkers suggested they take a trip to Morocco, he decided to go, and ended up spending two months in Morocco.

At one point, Alvaro found himself walking through the beautiful Sahara Desert. As he crossed the white sand, the thought occurred to him how happy he was he'd followed his heart and seized the opportunity to visit Europe. At that very moment, the wind blew over the dunes and he saw a shiny object in the sand. He bent down to pick it up. It was a golden key. What was such a key doing in the middle of nowhere? He immediately recognized that the universe was telling him: *The key to happiness is to follow your heart—* instead of being stopped by your fears.

He returned to Spain and one night while working at the bar, Alvaro met Jonathon, an older British man. Jonathon shared with him how he had once had a successful career with British Petroleum. Despite making exorbitant amounts of money, he had been unhappy. After his marriage fell apart, Jonathon resigned from BP, sold his home, and moved to a small island off the coast of Spain, where he worked as a golf instructor. He told Alvaro that he had no regrets and advised Alvaro to follow his dreams and never be afraid to take risks.

The two became good friends, and Jonathon offered Alvaro a job on this island paradise. Alvaro took the job and found himself working as an undocumented gardener in Europe, something he knew his family would find ironic. The ethnic stereotype of the undocumented Latino gardener haunted him, as did his self-criticism of this lifestyle of "restless aimlessness." Yet, Alvaro, had to admit to himself that he had never felt happier and more vibrant, joyful, and fulfilled.

When Alvaro finally returned to the United States, he found himself caught up in making a living to fulfill his family's expectation that he make good on the American Dream. The more he tried to fit into the middle-class mold, the more disconnected he became from himself, which led him to feeling depressed. It was then that he remembered the key and the conversation with Jonathon. He decided on a compromise. Figuring he'd have time to think and write, Alvaro gave notice at his job and returned to school.

People are always advising us to compromise. However, whenever we compromise ourselves, it doesn't work well in the long run. It's more of a delaying tactic. After three years, Alvaro left school and returned to his first love, something he had begun doing the moment his tiny hands were able to hold a pen—drawing. He loved to draw.

Alvaro's drawing led him to printmaking. He began making stunning carvings of the Salinas Valley where he grew up, along with prints of Día de los Muertos (Day of the Dead) images. Soon he was selling his print designs to tee-shirt companies, showing his art, and freelancing. While he was highly educated and could have chosen to pursue a number of traditional careers, he was most happy with a pen or print carving tool in his hand, surrounded by tiny wood shavings, a cup of coffee, and whoever showed up at the community table in the local café. This was his heart's desire. It was what made him come alive.

Living from the Inside Out

Alvaro and I talked about the ongoing need for him to address his fear that he was somehow not choosing a real career by being an artist. We discussed his inner dialogue, his self-talk, in which he disparaged himself. He spoke negatively about himself. This disempowered him. For instance, he sometimes referred to his art and his approach to life as this "hippie shit." He was torn about being working class versus middle class. Raised working class, but educated middle class, Alvaro didn't feel at home with either classes. He valued middle-class values, like art and education, but not middle-class materialism and ladder climbing.

I helped Alvaro recognize that he was a part of a new class of heart-based solopreneurs, modern renaissance men and women who are choosing their destinies rather than trying to fit themselves into prescribed roles.

When you play outside the established classes, their designations don't apply. You break with the old paradigm, not permitting yourself to be defined from the outside in, but instead living from the inside out. Living from the outside in consists of amassing outside approval and relying on it to help you feel good about yourself. In contrast, when you live from the inside out, you must generate your own certainty by learning to trust the universe as it expresses itself through you, allowing it to guide you.

Because of his strong family ties and foundational beliefs about class, Alvaro had to overcome the feeling that he was neither living up to his potential nor honoring the sacrifices made by his parents. I invited him to reframe what he was doing as a divine calling. I also urged him to consider the cost of not sharing gifts and talents that were unique to him. It wasn't uncommon for him to hear that his art evoked deep emotion in people. In fact, one of the first carvings he shared with me was of the Salinas Valley, and it was so beautiful that it brought tears to my eyes.

Alvaro needed more people in his life who, like Jonathon, could support him in listening to his inner wisdom when the pressures to conform amplified. He had connected with his heart's desires in Europe, then gotten disconnected from his heart. Reconnecting with his art helped him get back in touch with his heart and our conversations I believe allowed him to listen again to his inner wisdom. I was grateful our paths crossed when they did as his story was also a beautiful affirmation to me of my decision to keep following my heart.

A few years later I reconnected with Alvaro. He took a huge leap and is now studying at Cal State University's School of Art in Long Beach, working at the Los Angeles County Museum of Art and selling his artwork to collectors. Alvaro left something he was supposed to be doing to do something he needed to be doing.

As previously discussed, if you want to succeed and have the courage to pursue your authentic path, it's imperative you surround yourself with likeminded travelers who know the value of taking the journey of the courageous heart—people after your own heart, so to speak. Alvaro embodied the openheartedness and bravery of artists who share their creations raw and naked, to be examined by all.

Once you have made the decision to follow your heart, expect twists and turns. Don't expect the journey to be straightforward. Don't expect yourself to be perfect. You will have powerful experiences of connecting with your heart, your authentic center, and then you may still lose connection as that moment fades. You can't know upfront where all of this is going to take you. Sometimes your heart's desires change and expand. We are in a constant state of transformation. Be open and stay open. Let life lead. Keep finding ways to come back to your self.

The story of Alvaro illustrates beautifully how things unfold as we take one step at a time in response to our heart's prompting. Where those steps lead may surprise us.

Stay on the Train, Even If It Turns into a Roller Coaster

There's an excitement when you take those first steps on your journey to follow your heart and live your authentic life. Once you've taken those initial steps, it may seem as if nothing is happening or that everything is taking longer than expected.

Along the way, as change occurs, there will be situations in which you experience both highs and lows. At times your heart will ascend with the joys of heaven on earth and you will feel the delight of life's magic. Every flower, every blade of grass will be your beloved. But there will also be days of pure hell, when life's pain will cut you so deep that you'll believe you're being bled dry by grief.

Following your heart and living authentically isn't for people who want a predictable life. It's not for those who want to remain inside the lines or who need life to be steady. Keep in mind that on the EKG, a steady flat line indicates death. The electrocardiogram reading of a healthy heart resembles a rollercoaster. Lots of ups and downs. Following your heart is for those who are ready for the wild ride of transformation. The challenge is to stay committed, to stay on the ride. That's what it means to be your own hero. To do so requires you to build a strong heart muscle.

How do you do this?

Feel Your Feelings

Perhaps you are ahead of the curve and were given permission to feel your feelings as a child, or you've been able to give yourself permission as an adult. For others who were raised believing that feelings, especially sadness, make you weak, we learned it was better to suppress. We learned to stuff, sublimate, transmute, numb (through drink, food, or sex), or just plain ignore our feelings.

You can begin by noting where you feel the feelings in your body. Do you feel a tightness in your chest? A lump in your throat? A sick, knotted feeling in your stomach? Identify where the feelings are located in your body and then begin to name them. Are you feeling depression or just sadness? Lonely or alone? Abandoned or rejected? Confused or insecure? Are you feeling excited or nervous? Fearful or anxious? Try to discern the exact emotion you are experiencing.

Then, instead of resisting or fighting back feelings of sadness, despair, inadequacy, loss, abandonment, fear, rejection, envy, hopelessness, failure, or self-loathing, let those feelings come. Let them pass through like a rainstorm or a hurricane, feeling them in their totality. If you were raised to deny your feelings in one way or another, the prescription just to "feel 'em" may seem overwhelming. Yet, just feeling them, not trying to push them away or fix them, is the healthiest, strongest, most beneficial thing you can do for yourself.

Let the feelings come. Like storm clouds they will in due course pass through. Surrender your persona and mental survival strategies, and let the natural rhythms of the universe lead you. Once the emotional storm has ended, shore up what needs to be shored up and begin again. Nurture yourself during and after the storm, get support from friends and professionals, engage in self-love practices, and read things that inspire and uplift you. Then, allow the sun to come out again.

Also allow yourself to feel the good feelings on the other end the pendulum. Feel them fully and consciously. Learn to rejoice in what's truly another beautiful day in paradise. Instead of holding back, allow yourself to enjoy the beauty that surrounds you, love people deeply and tell them "I appreciate you." Not just people who you're physically intimate with, but friends and clients, and even people you meet in your daily life: your Lyft driver, the host at a restaurant, your hairdresser, and the baristas at your favorite café. Allow yourself to experience that inexplicable joy and amazement with life that's deep within each of us.

Go Have Fun

Sometimes the path forward is counterintuitive. Don't be surprised when this turns out to be the case! Paradoxically, one of the best things you can do for yourself when you start to feel stuck or enter into a mindset of scarcity is to go have fun. As a therapist, I feel like it's important to practice what you preach. The things I share with others, I've put into play for myself as I deal with my own life's challenges.

In September 2008, I gave three months' notice to leave my job as a psychologist for the Federal Bureau of Prisons. The next day, the U.S. government announced we were in a recession. Nevertheless, I chose to continue with my plan of building my own private practice. I was grateful that I'd saved money and could afford to take a little time to keep trusting the process. If you're going to start a business or quit your job, consider saving three to six months of living expenses before you do. This allows you to feel more comfortable and confident when you do take a calculated risk. Whatever you decide to do, remember, you're responsible for your choices.

At the end of my three months, I had two clients. In February, I was up to six. I was slowly building my practice. So slowly in fact, that my wife at the time was hoping I would go back to the prison if things didn't change.

Rather than stay home and indulge in worry and fear, which would only contract my energy and make me appear more desperate for clients, I decided to go on vacation. Solidly employed since I was sixteen, I had never gone for more than two weeks without a job or several jobs. I booked an inexpensive trip to Italy. Why stay home bored out of my mind waiting and hoping for clients to show up, when I could roam in Rome in the springtime? During my trip, I visited all the important tourist sites: the Vatican, the Sistine Chapel, the Jewish Ghetto, the Trevi Fountain. I even took a day trip to Pompeii. Travel is so good for the soul. It gets you out of your rut. Let me emphasize again, I took an inexpensive trip. This wasn't about wasting resources, it was about expanding my self-concept. It was about allowing myself to enjoy life.

I'm not suggesting that everyone should take an international vacation when they're out of work and money is tight. However, when you begin contracting in fear, you can find simple ways to have fun. Take a beach day or go for a drive in the country. Go to the movies or have lunch with a friend. Find a way to have fun, to stay light and open, so you don't freak out and become overwhelmed with rigidity and fear.

After I returned from Rome, rather than seeing my lack of clients as a failure, I saw the emptiness in my schedule as the gift I'd yearned for. Instead of spending my days worrying about getting more clients, I began writing my second book. If I'd succumbed to fear I would have frittered the time away, grasping for clients.

During that time, I dragged out my old Tony Robbins *Powertalk* cassette tapes and listened to them as I drove to the café to write. The *Powertalk* audio program was recorded in 1992 and talked about a horrible recession the country was in. *There was a recession in 1992?* I had no idea. I was in my first year of graduate studies at the time and had no awareness of the country's economic concerns. Listening to people talk about the 1992 recession and how they thought it was the end of the world gave me hope. The current recession couldn't last forever. On the tapes, people shared how they made themselves immune to the 1992 recession. They emphasized the importance of being flexible and making peace with change.

I felt so empowered that I pulled the application for a full-time job as a professor that I had applied for in February when things were looking bleak—a position that was practically guaranteed to me. At any other time in my life, it would have been the perfect job for me. I had enjoyed over ten years of teaching masters level psych students at that university, and it was only a five-minute drive from my house. However, now I felt that the job would be too small for me. I was committed to growing my own business and forging my own path. Even though I couldn't see the clients who were going to come to me, I felt deep in my heart that it was better to release this job opportunity rather than releasing my dream. I shifted my focus.

Choose Your Focus

What are you focusing your attention on? Are you looking for evidence you will fail, or uplifting yourself by focusing on what's going well in your life and being open to positive possibilities?

When I quit my job at the beginning of the recession, I could have focused on the tight economy and told myself I was going to fail, I'd never find clients and no one would pay my private practice fees. I even heard of established psychologists cutting their rates. I couldn't believe it. At a party, one guy told me he couldn't get anybody to work with him because therapy was a luxury. I knew this was untrue because I had a friend who had a waiting list. Instead of focusing on how hard it was to build a practice, I focused on her. I listened to successful people and what they had to say, which helped awaken my own successful nature. By the summer, I had more clients.

During the recession I invested in myself. In August 2009, I enrolled in a business coaching program that focused on client attraction. I began learning how to share with people ways I could help them with therapy and coaching, something I was never taught in my expensive psychology doctoral program. With some new knowledge on marketing myself in a sincere way, my practice began to take off. I learned some skills and as I grew so did my clientele.

Then I invested time creating new coaching groups and programs like my *How to Come Out of the Closet and Into Your Power!* audio program to help LGBT people love and accept themselves. Equality and self-acceptance are two values I'm extremely passionate about. I stayed focused on thriving, despite the recession. I traveled to small towns and offered free "coming out" workshops to LGBT people in rural communities. I began coaching clients in other countries dealing with coming out and gender transitioning, and supporting people who previously lacked access to these kinds of services. One of my biggest joys was hosting a free coming out teleseminar in which people in four different countries participated—the United States, Canada, Korea, and Australia.

What we think about, what we pay attention to, and what we talk about show us if we are approaching life from our essential essence, or whether we are mired in the negativity of our head or the contagion of race consciousness—the perceptions of fear, lack, and scarcity promulgated by our news sources. Knowing that in our deepest being we are naturally positive, we can utilize a trifecta of positive emotion—by shifting our thoughts, focus, and speech—that will help us express the good feeling of our essence. This, in turn, will energize us to go after our goals, since when we feel good, we tap into the resilience needed to move through what we think is rejection and on to the next opportunity. We find ourselves flowing past obstacles, on toward the manifestation of our heart's desires.

On the other hand, we can hit the losing trifecta if we allow ourselves to be taken over by negative thoughts that lead us to focus on what's not going well in our life and cause us to speak about ourselves and our situation with disappointment or even self-deprecation.

Turn your attention away from the problems and the disappointments in your life or in your interactions with others. Notice what *is* working for you—the things that are going smoothly, the opportunities right under your nose, the good things that are happening in your life that you likely aren't noticing because you've been on autopilot and have taken these things for granted.

You can find abundance by focusing on the fact you still have enough to eat, friends who love you, clean water, your abilities (vision, hearing, speech), your education (formal and the things you've learned from life). Even though you may not be making the kind of money you'd like to make, you still have an abundance of fresh air to breathe. You may also have access to nature, books, and the internet (which allows us to learn almost anything). If time is a limited resource, just take five minutes to sit in silence or to sip a cup of tea. Taking time to appreciate the little things really does matter in the big picture.

Learn to Look for the Good

While I was coaching Liz, a professional comedian and actor, she brought up how she *wanted* her career to look, in contrast to what it seemed like at that moment. The TV show she was on wanted to write more acting parts for her. Because the show's skits didn't fit with the roles she envisioned for herself, Liz was less than thrilled. She was frustrated that her agent hadn't booked more guest spots for her on other shows.

I asked Liz to focus on her *actual* successes instead of what she imagined her TV career *ought* to be. Up until this moment, most of what Liz thought about and talked about was how far she hadn't come in her career. She had been focused on what *wasn't* happening rather than on the acting/performing opportunities that *were*. All of this was coming from her head, not her heart. She realized that what was right in front of her was as good as getting small parts as guests on other shows. The good was right there, but she hadn't seen it. The writers for this show were writing roles *specifically for her* because they loved her.

Does this happen in your life? Is it happening now? Are you not seeing or appreciating what's right under your nose? If you were to look for the good, what could you begin to appreciate in your life? Can you begin to see the good in yourself, and recognize your own positive contributions to the world?

Paradoxically, the more Liz saw the good in her life, the more opportunities opened up for her. The universe likes it when we appreciate it. So, the more we bless those good things that show up in our lives, the more the universe wants to give us the goods. This is the metaphysical meaning of biblical passages like Luke 12:32, "It is God's good pleasure to give you the kingdom,"[1] and Matthew 13:12, "Whoever has will be given more."[2] To those who are grateful and see the good in what's already in their lives, Luke 19:26 says, "More will be given."[3] Remember, the more we see the good in our lives, feel gratitude, and express appreciation, the more magnetic we are to more good.

Shawn Achor, author of *The Happiness Advantage*, spent several years at Harvard University studying the empirical evidence for the connection between happiness and business success. His research found that happiness fuels success and work productivity, a phenomenon he called the *happiness advantage*. People who are happy perform better and have more success in business.[4] Achor encourages people not to pin their happiness on success, but to find ways to feel happy now, which, in turn, will lead to greater success.

Once again, I cannot emphasize enough that you aren't *creating* a good feeling by telling yourself positive things. Rather, you are recognizing *what's already true*. The more frequently you make this choice, the more your true self will spring to life, enabling you to surf the waves of change and enjoy the process.

In the next chapter, we will dive into how to create a sense of certainty in the face of the unknown and relax into the flow of life.

INVITATION

Today, choose to keep your focus trained on the good things. Look for the good. Focus on what is going right. View challenges as part of the adventure. See yourself working through the challenges and becoming stronger and more flexible, building confidence, and developing an ability to ride the rollercoaster of life with greater joy and less trepidation.

CHAPTER SEVENTEEN

Keep the Faith and Follow the Flow

"I think the most important question facing humanity is, 'Is the universe a friendly place?' This is the first and most basic question all people must answer for themselves."
—*Albert Einstein*

As you take steps to live a life that is authentic and honors your true self, it's important to have faith. Our English word *faith* comes from the Latin word *fides*, which means "to trust, to have confidence in." Faith involves listening to your heart's calling, entrusting yourself to this beckoning by taking steps in the direction of your desires, being willing to take intuitive risks, and thereby living a life that truly honors your spirit and heart.

As poet Patrick Overton said, "When you walk to the edge of all the light you have and take that first step into the darkness of the unknown, you must believe that one of two things will happen. There will be something solid for you to stand upon or you will be taught to fly."[1]

Taking steps in the direction of your inner calling is easier if you believe in a friendly universe that supports you. If you think the world is a hostile, dog-eat-dog place, you'll be more reluctant to answer the call, especially when you're asked to let go and trust. However, if you can just "act as if" and take a step, then the next step, then the next, you'll find that the universe makes a way for you. This is the message that is shared in Jewish homes every Passover when the story of the Hebrew slaves fleeing Egypt is retold.

The Hebrews were slaves in Egypt. They escaped as far as the Red Sea, but they had no way to cross and the Pharaoh's soldiers were right behind them. Some chose to give up hope at that moment and turned back toward Egypt. But one man, Nahshon, began walking into the water. He trusted that if God told Moses the people would be free, God would make a way where no way seemed possible. He walked in up to his nose as the story is told. When the water filled Nahshon's nostrils and he was about to drown, the waters began to part. The Hebrews made it across the sea to freedom.

Many mystics and metaphysicians believe that the Passover miracle is a metaphor for the power of our own beliefs to move figurative mountains and part figurative seas. Miracles can occur in our own lives when we stay on the path of faith and trust in the goodness of the universe. It's also a reminder that we will face obstacles, things will look impossible at times, and we must keep moving forward, committed to our vision, even when appearances would tell us that it's a hopeless cause.

"Don't give up five minutes before the miracle," they say in Alcoholics Anonymous meetings. I know you've also heard the aphorism, "It's always darkest before the dawn." I've certainly experienced the truth of both of these statements, as have countless of my clients. I also believe that, intuitively, we know these things to be true.

Surely this is why the formula that undergirds any good novel or movie involves taking the protagonist on a hero's journey in which life is comfortable and might even be about to get better, when something bad happens and things get worse. Right when things look like they might be about to improve for our hero, everything falls apart and it looks like all hope is lost. It's only when the protagonist has scraped the bottom of the barrel that things gradually change and the journey ends with a new kind of good—a new normal.

So, even as the hero's journey in story form goes from good, then to bad, then to horrible, and then to a new kind of good, your journey of the courageous heart may take this course too. This is why you must stay your course and find your faith.

Deep within, all of us sense that when we choose to follow our hearts, we are in the embrace of the Divine. No matter how dark it may be at this moment, your deeper self knows that the sun will rise and shine on your life again— with one difference. You will have become a deeper, richer, more fulfilled individual in the process, capable of so much more than you were before the crisis you've gone through began.

Your inner being is trusting by nature. Here are some simple steps to help you lean in to that place of trust. First, sit quietly. Next, take some deep relaxing breathes in through your nose and out through your nose. Quiet and relax the mind and body. Soften your focus by just bringing your focus to your breath. Allow a deeper meditative state to envelop you. It's easier to find your faith in this place, rather than in the chaos or chatter of the outside world. Your faith lies within.

Some practices that I employ with my clients to increase a sense of tangible faith include connecting with the power of words. Some helpful phrases I encourage them to repeat to themselves are:

- "I trust life."
- "I allow myself to be at peace."
- "I am willing to trust in a friendly Universe."
- "I allow life to support me."

We have the ability to impact our lives with our thoughts and our words. Thoughts like *My life is working out for me* create a positive anticipation toward the future. While thoughts like *Nothing ever works out for me* or *There is no point in trying* darken our view of the future. Words like *harmony* and *joy* evoke positive feelings, while words like *chaos* and *rage* evoke more negative feeling states. I believe we can use words to shift our moods which will shift our thoughts. We can use words to create hope or we can use them to create despair.

I mentioned using affirmations to increase your feelings of self-love in Chapter 10, "Nurture Your Authentic Self."

Affirmations can also help us elevate our mood and connect with a faith in ourselves and the future.

Affirmations aren't going to magically change your life by asserting something to be true. You can't just think or speak your dreams into existence. A scene from the Academy Award-winning 1999 film *American Beauty* comes to mind. We see Annette Benning playing Carolyn Burnham, a real estate agent who, as she walks through the front door of a home she's listing, exclaims, "I will sell this house today." Later, we see her maniacally cleaning the house, washing windows, sweeping the floors, dusting the fan, and vacuuming the floor, affirming with ever greater force, "I will sell this house today."

Finally, we see her staring at herself in the mirror exclaiming through tightened lips, "I will sell this house today." But in the end, she doesn't sell the house.[2]

Affirmations are not a magical panacea for all your challenges. They don't negate the laws of the physical world. If you affirm you can fly and then jump off a bridge, the law of gravity will far outweigh the law of attraction.

Benning's character could have employed an affirmation such as "I will do my best today. I will trust that the right buyers will come at the right time. I know that everything is working together for my highest good." When we use affirmations in this realistic way, it can help us feel better about ourselves and our lives, more intentional and focused, and this will increase our resilience and willingness to continue to pursue our dreams in the face of inevitable setbacks.

As Dr. Amy Cuddy suggests in her book *Presence*, statements that affirm things we already believe about ourselves can increase our confidence. Affirmations such as "I am a hard worker. I am a good friend. I am a college graduate. I show up and do my best," can increase our self-esteem *if they are true*. By contrast, statements that are trying to affirm something that may not be true, like "I am the President of the United States. I make a billion dollars a year. I am going to win the lottery," will have less impact on our self-esteem and confidence.

Additionally, affirmations that use words that evoke a powerful positive vibration can uplift us. For example, "I am loved. Life is for me. I am cherished. I am a good person." These statements can create positive feelings, especially when spoken aloud.

I recommend clients create empowering affirmations and then write them in a journal and get into the habit of reading their affirmations and ideally saying them out loud, at least once a week. My clients tell me that when they do this they feel better. In most instances, reading their true affirmations will shift them out of a depressed or anxious mood into one that is helpful and motivating. One reason they feel better is because they connect with statements that at one point they knew were true, but forgot or lost connection with because of previous disappointments or the blanket of pessimism that accompanies depression. After affirming positive statements that are true about themselves, they begin to see possibilities rather than remaining mired in negative self-evaluation. They feel more hopeful about their lives and their circumstances after connecting with their affirmations. It's not that they are suddenly caught up in magical thinking that they are going to be on *The Oprah Show* or become billionaires, but they are empowered to take tangible steps toward their goals, like practicing their guitar, getting back to their writing, or approaching their business or their job with a fresh enthusiasm. As Woody Allen is quoted to have said, "Eighty percent of success is showing up."[3]

There is another practice that takes affirmations one step further: spiritual mind treatment (SMT), which is also known as affirmative prayer. SMT is typically associated with metaphysically oriented new thought spiritual traditions, such as Centers for Spiritual Living, Unity, and Divine Science. It is a prayer technique in which a positive affirmation is made asserting that something is already done. Examples would include:

- "I affirm that John's surgery is successful and he recovers fully from his condition."
- "I affirm that all of Monica's bills are paid."
- "I know Laura's home is sold at the right price and at the right time. All of the details are managed from the right buyers, to ease and grace with moving out and the close of escrow."

When I'm doing spiritual counseling sessions, SMT is an important part of the session. Some of my coaching and therapy clients also find SMT useful and may ask me to devise a unique mind treatment for their situation. As with anything, if this practice appeals to you, then try it out. If it doesn't, that's okay too.

Below is the formula for a spiritual mind treatment as suggested by twentieth-century new thought spiritual teacher and writer Ernest Holmes, founder of Science of Mind, with an additional step of gratitude that was introduced by contemporary new thought spiritual teacher, Michael Bernard Beckwith.

HOW TO DO A SPIRITUAL MIND TREATMENT

A spiritual mind treatment or affirmative prayer begins with a moment of silence and with a few deep breaths to create sacred space. It can be spoken with the eyes open or closed, though eyes closed is usually preferred. It can be spoken in your mind or said aloud. It can be written. Personally, I believe speaking your SMT aloud is more powerful.

Step 1. First, you begin with gratitude. You state what you are grateful for.

Example: "I give thanks for this beautiful day. For the sunshine, the trees, the breath in my lungs, the roof over my head, the food in my stomach. I am thankful for my fingers and toes, for the beating of my heart, for my friends and family."

Step 2. The second step is recognizing the field of Love (Energy, Presence, God, Life, the Divine), that surrounds us. We acknowledge the unified field, the Universe, whatever it is we call the ineffable and the qualities of this presence.

All you essentially need is a belief that there is a presence in the universe that's good, ordered, and working on your behalf. When you tap into this presence and affirm what your heart is asking of you, it will equip you with whatever may be required to deliver your dream. As for the exact words, it doesn't matter what you call this presence: Love, Source, Great Spirit, Beloved One, Creator, God, Goddess, Universe, Infinite Intelligence, Allah, Adonai, Great Mystery, Mother-Father, Presence, Shekinah, Life, the One, Eloheinu, Hashem, Higher Power, the Way, Perfect Pattern, Mother Nature, the Force. Call it whatever you feel you want to call It. Since it's all-knowing and all-seeing, It will answer your call in the best ways, at the best time, and for the highest good of all.

Example: "I recognize that there is only One, one unified field, one power, one presence, and that presence is love, beauty, divine intelligence, grace, life itself. *It* is all powerful, all knowing, all seeing, everywhere present. *It* has no ending and no beginning. *It* is the allness of life itself, the creator of all beingness." (Swap your preferred term for the italicized word *It*.)

Step 3. The third step is unifying ourselves with our higher presence, with the Universe.

Example: "I affirm that I am one with all that is. One with the One. One with life itself. One with beauty, one with truth, one with wholeness. I know that I am made in the image and likeness of this perfect presence. I am one with God."

Step 4. The fourth step is *realization*. In this step, we speak our affirmative prayer, affirming the condition we are seeking to know the truth of. We state it as if what we are praying for is already done. This step is most powerful when we affirm general qualities, rather than specific demands. For example, instead of praying for Mark or Mary to love us. We affirm that we are always *loved*. Instead of affirming a relationship with Mark or Mary, we affirm that we are always in the *divine right relationship* or *the perfect relationship for us*.

It is better for us to affirm positive qualities, like happiness, love, abundance, divine right expression of our gifts and talents, divine right livelihood, and so on, than trying to pray for specific things that we believe will make us happy, specific people we want to attract, or specific sums of money, salaries, or jobs.

If you don't like the word *divine*, simply remove it and keep the word *right* in front of your affirmation.

Example: "I know that everything is working together for my highest good. I claim divine/*right* action in my life where my employment is concerned. I know the perfect opportunities come to me with ease and grace that utilize my gifts and talents for the greatest good. I know that all of my needs are met. My bills are taken care of and I live in the overflow. I know divine/*right* relationships in my life. I know the Universe has chosen the perfect companion for me. I know that I am always loved."

As you can see, this is a very different prayer than "God give me . . ." and different than making a specific demand of the Universe. This approach works best when we are willing to surrender the details to a higher power.

When you are in crisis around a health condition, or someone else is, you could do a SMT like this. "I know that the love, the peace, the protection of God surrounds Isaac/*me*. I know that Isaac has/*I have* all that Isaac needs/*I need* to move through this situation. I know that regardless of appearances everything is working together for Isaac's/*my* highest good. I know that the hand of the Divine moves through every nurse and doctor who cares for Isaac/*me*."

A spiritual mind treatment for the possibility of losing your home to foreclosure could include the following: "I know that I am always guided, guarded, directed, and protected. I know that I am at home in the Universe and the Universe will always provide for me. I know that regardless of appearance everything is working together for my highest good. I trust that if this home is meant to be released that there is another divine idea for my home."

I realize that this is not as comforting to some as being able to say, "I know that my house won't be foreclosed on." However, we can't know that for sure, so a prayer like, "I will always have shelter as needed. I trust the Divine to provide shelter for me in ways that are for my highest good. I am open and available to be shown the perfect dwelling for me at this time," will be more effective.

A prayer like this allows the Universe to work with you. For example, one of my friends and writing clients, Celeste, was looking for a new home for her family because their landlord didn't renew her lease. She and her family had to move out of the home they'd been in for almost ten years. The house she'd brought her babies home to. It would have been a waste to affirm "we don't have to move." Instead, she used affirmative prayer to know that the perfect home for her family was already known by Spirit—her term.

Celeste and her husband were unable to find an apartment to rent that met their needs by the end of the lease. One of Celeste's friends had a furnished apartment that was going to be empty for the summer and offered it to Celeste. Celeste knew this was part of Spirit's plan and received this offer with an open heart and mind.

Celeste and her husband moved their belongings into storage and moved into the friend's apartment complex, which had a pool and was close to the ocean. Her kids were thrilled. They continued to look for a place to live. She found another apartment that would be available at the end of summer and was perfect for the family. It was also close to the ocean and had a pool. Celeste and her family moved into the new apartment right before the kids started school. It was perfect for them.

A few years later, Celeste and her husband separated. Celeste found another apartment in the same complex so that her kids could easily go back and forth between her new place and the old apartment where their dad remained. The Universe knew the perfect home for this family for all its incarnations.

When we let go and trust the Universe to provide for us we are allowing ourselves to be led by a power greater than ourselves that knows best how to fit all the puzzle pieces together. This doesn't mean we do nothing, it means that we stay open, we don't insist rigidly that things look a certain way.

Here's another example. Suppose you have a test coming up. You've studied and know the course material, but you still have test anxiety and are afraid of flunking. Faith means you affirm that you know everything you need to know to pass this test. You affirm that you have the mental and emotional ability to pass. You affirm that you've already completed this test and have received a passing grade. You might even visualize your paper with a passing grade on it and allow yourself to feel what it's like to receive such a grade. You are affirming *faith in the divinely given vision and the work you've done to turn the vision into a reality.*

Step 5. The fifth step is giving thanks that what you have affirmed, or treated for, has been provided. You're paying forward the gratitude.

Example: "Thank you, Beloved Universe, for bringing the perfect job/clients, home, love, into my life. Thank you for connecting me with wonderful friends. Thank you for restoring my health. Thank you for watching over my children and providing them with a fantastic education."

Step 6. The sixth and final step is to release the affirmative prayer into the Universe. This is the letting go and letting God step.

Example: "I release this prayer into the Universe. And so it is." Or: "I release my word into the loving care of God. And so it is."

Or, more formally: "I release my word into the law, knowing that the law always says yes. And so it is. Amen."

A spiritual mind treatment is like sowing seeds. You prepare the soil, dig the hole, plant the seed, cover it up, water it, and then leave it be. You don't dig a seed up to see if it's growing. You let it go and let it grow.

Spiritual mind treatments (affirmative prayers) are a means of aligning ourselves with the intelligence of the Universe that dwells in our inner being, our essential self. When what we want to create in our life flows from this heart center, we take the kind of action that we are being prompted to take by the divine wisdom that's our birthright—and sometimes that action is simply to wait and let life bring us, perhaps not what we want, but what we need and is for our highest good and ultimate happiness.

If the practice of spiritual mind treatment doesn't resonate with you, experiment and find what does. It's a practice my clients find useful and I recommend as one of the tools you can use to keep yourself strong on the journey.

Staying Aligned with Your Good

Katheryn Elizabeth Hudson was raised in a very religious household in Santa Barbara, California. As a little girl she wasn't allowed to watch the Smurfs, which her parents considered satanic, or listen to secular music. Her parents were traveling ministers and she traveled with them singing church songs from the age of nine when she also began taking voice lessons. She loved music and wrote her own songs. When she was fifteen, her talents were discovered by professional musicians who saw her potential. They connected her with people in the Nashville music scene who mentored her in song writing and guitar lessons. At sixteen, she released a gospel album, entitled *Katy Hudson*. The album tanked, selling only one hundred copies.

Sometimes we may appear to fail at something because something even bigger and better is waiting for us. While Katy's impact on the Christian rock scene was pretty uneventful, she caught the attention of Columbia Records. It looked like Katy's career was picking up. They had a vision for her and wanted to sculpt her look and her music, making her more like Avril Lavigne and other successful female musicians of the time. Katy had another vision for herself and her music, something less moody and more empowering. Columbia wasn't into it and they dropped her. Her dream was slipping through her fingers. Already she was getting a reputation as the female musician dropped by multiple record labels.

In 2007, at twenty-three years old, she signed with Capitol Records under the name Katy Perry, though she was still on the proverbial backburner. One of the songs she wrote met with great resistance from the record company and they didn't even want to put the song on her album. They believed the song was too controversial and wouldn't get played on the radio. Again, Katy was bumping heads with the people who had the power to bring her vision to life. Despite the expectations of conventional wisdom, a radio station in Nashville, Tennessee, known for being conservative and anti-gay, agreed to play the song. They played the song for three days and according to one spokesperson for Capitol Records, they were "inundated with enthusiastic calls" and requests for what would become Katy Perry's first international chart topping single, "I Kissed a Girl!" This song that almost didn't make it on to the album ended up being one of the best-selling singles worldwide and launched Perry's career.[4] Being your authentic self is always an alchemical recipe for success!

If we take Katy Perry's story and provide the thought soundtrack, or internal dialogue, to her career it might sound like this: "It's okay that my gospel album only sold one hundred copies, as in my heart I know this market is too small for me. I'm meant to play bigger stages than even the biggest mega-church can provide me. My audience is a worldwide audience, not limited to Christian listeners or Christian themes. I'm thankful that I'm not trapped by the Christian rock scene where I would only be playing it safe anyway."

Dropped by Island Def Jam and Columbia Records. "The Universe is so smart. It knows that the ways the music producers were trying to market me, and change me, would not allow me to bring out my true gifts and talents. They saw me as small. They wanted me to be someone else. I know that I am perfect as I am. I know that I am a great musician, performer, and songwriter in my own right. Soon the world will know that too and the music producers who gave me a record contract are going to be glad I signed with them."

Controversy over the song "I Kissed a Girl." "I know that the Universe put this song in my head because I am the right performer to sing this song and now is the right time to sing it. I trust and know that there is an audience out there of people who are hungry for what I have to share. I am willing to be their voice."

These are the ways we want to talk to ourselves. As Katy suggests in her song "Firework," we may want to remind ourselves that just because one door is closed to us, doesn't mean that a window isn't going to open up somewhere else. Who needs doors when the perfect road awaits you?

Go with the Flow

One of the most important ways to keep your heart open and trust the Universe is to go with the flow. When we let go of trying to make things go in a certain direction or to a particular schedule—when we no longer demand that situations work out in the way we think they should—the universe will guide us in an even better way than we can imagine. It's crucial that we learn to *allow and accept*.

Instead of dictating how things should go, simply be aware of what doors are open. Notice the invitations you receive. Pay attention to which paths seem to lead to dead-ends and brick walls, and which ones continue to expand. This is a time of deep listening to your inner wisdom.

We must always remain open to how our waking dreams might take shape, an availability that requires freeing ourselves from the tendency to become attached to a particular outcome. When we let go of attachment to how it should be and follow the love, follow the flow, life's beauty opens up to us.

In the next chapter, we will discuss how to let go of the old and open to the new life that is waiting to emerge through us.

INVITATION

Invite the Universe to be a part of your journey. Imagine, for even just one day, that the Universe is friendly and working for your good. Your *good*, not your wish list. Trust that whatever unfolds today is connected to something greater. Be available to the flow of life and how it wants to unfold for you today. Enter the stillness and listen deeply to where your soul is leading you today.

CHAPTER EIGHTEEN

Expect and Respect Your Metamorphosis

"Anytime we update our lives, we have to grieve for the old life that's been lost."
—Christiane Northrup

L oss is an inevitable part of change and growth. We may choose change as part of following our courageous hearts. Or change can be forced on us, as in the case of being fired or laid off, going through a divorce, experiencing failing health, or having a loved one die.

Whether change chooses us or we choose change so we may lead a more authentic life and follow our heart's calling, the loss is still real.

We may feel a greater sense of empowerment in being the one choosing the ending—for instance, giving your notice versus getting laid off. While removing the element of surprise by choosing the change may lessen the discomfort, you may still have to work through feelings of self-doubt, regret, and possibly guilt associated with being the instigator.

William Bridges, psychologist and author of *Transitions*, identifies three psychological phases people go through when facing change. He calls them the "ending," the "neutral zone," and the "new beginning."[1]

In the first phase, the *ending*, we say goodbye to jobs, lovers, spouses, homes, an old identity, or whatever it is that's ending or we're letting go of. We leave our comfort zone.

Once we've experienced the ending of a situation, we find ourselves in the *neutral zone*, which Bridges describes as the "betwixt and between place." We aren't who we were, but we haven't yet become who we will be either. We are without the comfort of our old identity, surroundings, and sense of mastery, and yet our new self—with its roles, possibly a new physical location, and our changed social and emotional context—hasn't yet gelled. Although the old way doesn't work anymore, we haven't figured out a system for mastering the new.

Bridges says that during this period we must surrender to the process of disintegration. He explains that it's "only by returning for a time to the formlessness of the primal energy that renewal can take place."[2]

During this phase of transition, Bridges recommends we find significant time to be alone so that "inner signals can make themselves heard."[3] He also recommends that the neutral zone is a good time to go on a personal retreat. During this retreat, you might spend some time writing your autobiography and discovering what you really want out of life.

This period of change resembles the caterpillar in the pupa or chrysalis stage of development. No longer a caterpillar, and still far from spreading its wings to fly, the entity that will become the butterfly is in a betwixt and between stage. This is a vulnerable moment, in which powerful processes are acting on this tiny creature, shaping it to become what it's meant to be. But first the caterpillar liquefies completely so that it is totally shapeless, waiting to be reformed.

As we leave the comfort zone of our persona or constructed self to reclaim our authentic self, a parallel psychological transformation unfolds. We may enter into a stage of ambiguity and uncertainty. While our physical body may remain unchanged, it's quite possible that how we identify ourselves, who we know ourselves to be, completely evaporates. This can be frightening if we don't understand what's happening and how necessary this process is.

We will likely experience this stage as one of confusion, uncertainty, and mourning. We are not in a place to create our new identity, let alone our new beginning.

Spiritual teacher Michael Bernard Beckwith comments insightfully:

The butterfly does not contradict the caterpillar; it is a stage of unfoldment. At some point the caterpillar surrenders to the impulse of transforming into a butterfly. When the evolutionary impulse begins to cause you to want to scratch its itch, you will know it.

You don't have to feel anxious about surrendering to it.
Allow it. Surrender is simply saying, "I am available to
what seeks to emerge through and as me."[4]

Betwixt and Between

My client, Zoe, found herself in a betwixt and between phase after her marriage ended. She'd married later in life and postponed having children. She and her husband had struggled with fertility issues and he had finally given up. Every plan she had laid out for herself evaporated. The life she had outlined for herself in detail—staying home and raising children—vanished and with it her sense of self and self-worth.

She didn't know what to do with her weekends, let alone her life. Nevertheless, Zoe tried to figure out what step to take next. She considered adoption or fostering a child, but that seemed wrong. She felt clear that she didn't want to marry again. Nothing in her life made any sense. Now free to do whatever she wanted to do, she had no idea what she wanted.

Rather than trying to find an action to take, or a direction to go in, I invited Zoe to take some time before making any major decisions. She was in the neutral zone. It was not time to figure out next steps, it was a time to be still and wait.

If you didn't choose the change in your life, you may blame yourself. You may feel depressed and possibly even suicidal. You may feel unlucky and victimized by life. If you are choosing change, at some point on the path you might find yourself asking, "Why did I choose this path? Why couldn't I have just been happy with my old life? How come I chose to leave those comfortable aspects of that life for this?" You may ask, "WTF?" (Why trust faith?) "How can I be still and wait?" Personally, I believe this time of crisis is perfect for soul-searching.

You may find yourself completely stuck. You may even have to take actions that look like you're going backward or worse. *It's not a failure unless you decide it is.* Don't berate yourself if you have to move back in with your parents, find yourself couch surfing, or have to opt for some less desirable compromise. The Universe is making preparations for you. Everything happens for a reason, and no, it's not because you're a schmuck.

The more you can surrender by engaging in practices that focus on inner peace, self-acceptance, and self-care, the more resilient you will feel regardless of how long it takes for this uncomfortable period to pass.

I experienced this after my former wife, Molly, and I separated. I moved into a friend's basement apartment, temporary quarters just for the summer, or so I thought. My life was in a holding pattern. I had too much time on my hands and so much freedom that I didn't know what to do with myself. When you lose a whole community of friends, a house that requires upkeep, pets that need to be fed, and other routines and rituals that are both familiar and comforting, life is different.

I journeyed into the great unknown of whom I was to become, I knew it had something to do with following my spiritual calling. This calling was something I sensed instinctively but couldn't articulate—it was unformed. I knew I had to surrender.

I felt the confusion and frustration of the between and betwixt stage acutely. I deeply resented the holding pattern. It made me feel weak! I wanted to be through it, on the other side, creating a new comfort zone from a fresh beginning. I wanted to start building my life again. However, you can't build when you are neither caterpillar nor butterfly, but a sack of mush in the process of transformation. I had no feet to walk on, yet I desperately wanted wings that would allow me to gracefully transcend my current circumstances of living in a basement apartment. I was unable to write, unable to move forward.

I resented the neutral zone.

This was when I learned a new word, *chemicalization*. It's a spiritual term that was introduced by Christian Scientist Mary Baker Eddy, who defined it as the "upheaval produced when immortal truth is destroying erroneous mortal belief."[5] She also referred to it as a process "forcing impurities to pass away, as in the case with fermenting fluid."[6]

My life was in the process of spiritual chemicalization.

Going through the process of ending my marriage, I was being purified. To mix several metaphors in order to make my point, any aspects of my life that didn't serve my soul's higher purpose were being cooked out. All things egoic were being forced into the light. In other words, anything that wasn't for my highest good was rising to the surface like a rash of whitehead pimples.

On a purely practical level, clothes no longer fit. Items I treasured no longer made sense in my life. I was left with boxes of stuff I didn't know what to do with. They had made sense in my old world and lacked context in my new world. Music I'd loved, I could no longer bear to hear. I reached back to the time before my marriage. *Who was I? Who had I been?* I tried to reconnect with that person, but she wasn't there either.

At the time, I was involved in a deeply introspective spiritual program in which we were regularly reflecting on our lives—where we'd been and what had brought us to our current circumstances. One of the exercises was to write our own obituary, then create and conduct a memorial service for ourselves. To sum up the past forty years of my life and all the ways I had contributed to the communities I was connected with was a profoundly unsettling experience.

As I embarked on this assignment, I realized I was at a serious crossroads in my life. This meant I found it difficult to imagine what the next five years would look like, let alone the next forty. Consequently, I had the sense that I truly was giving a memorial service for the me who had once been.

New Beginnings

In the third phase of a transition of great magnitude, we find ourselves accepting the change that has taken place and in turn creating what Bridges refers to as the *new beginning*.

We learn the rules of this new place, recreating ourselves, drawing new people and new opportunities to us. We start developing new rituals, new routines.

After a year in the basement apartment, I needed to get my physical and emotional bearings and start over. I moved to Los Angeles. That was my new beginning.

In Los Angeles, I established new rituals. I found coffee shops to write in and I shed my San Francisco Bay Area professional look for shorts, flip-flops, and clothes that matched the perpetual summer vibe of LA. I even shaved my head.

I felt like I wasn't me anymore. Here I was choosing a life of courageous authenticity, yet I didn't even feel comfortable in my own clothes, let alone my own skin. In this stage of transition, I felt far from the person I wanted to become.

My life resembled a forest floor scorched by fire. Over time, seedlings began to appear, harbingers of the forest that was to follow. I still felt overwhelmed when I surveyed the landscape of what my life had once been, a growing sense of comfort gave me hope that I could move through the heartbreak of the ending of my old life.

For my client Nancy, her new beginning came when she moved out of the house in the suburbs she'd shared for thirty-five years with her husband after she decided she'd rather be alone than continue to share him with other women. She relocated to a condo in a nearby city. In our work together, she focused on grieving her losses and building a new life. She decided to volunteer at an animal shelter where she began to make new friends since she'd lost many of her couple friends in the divorce.

Dealing with Loss

How we cope with change and loss impacts our happiness, emotional and physical wellbeing, and continued willingness to grow by making changes, taking risks, and thereby stepping out of our comfort zone and control zone.

In our journey to greater authenticity, we may lose aspects of a former identity and experience significant changes. Our ego undergoes a death. Not only do we experience the loss of ways of knowing ourselves, we also let go of people, places, routines, all of which evoke grief.

Anytime we leave a dead-end job or end a long-term relationship, our decision is bound to trigger other people's unresolved issues. We may lose friends who no longer understand or respect the choices we are making. Often, we frighten them by inadvertently bringing them face to face with their own issues. It's not that we are bad, and it's not that what they are feeling is wrong. Simply put, our decisions have a way of rocking other people's boats even when this is the last thing we would wish.

While we aren't responsible for other people's reactions, their reactions to our actions may impact us. For example, like Nancy found, if we've socialized with others as part of a couple, and we end the relationship, other couples may now find our singleness disconcerting. Though we didn't intend such, our new course in life becomes a threat to their relationship. When this occurs, we may realize it wasn't us they were socializing with or enjoying a friendship with, but the merger of us and our partner. Now that we are no longer partnered, and the social unit they once related to is no more, they may not invite us over or wish to socialize with us. The friendship dissolves. This might also occur when we have kids or leave a job or organization, since the social contract is broken and there may be little common territory. Additionally, our identity is shifting, so that we no longer fit with all the other pieces of the puzzle.

We may minimize the loss. Perhaps we tell ourselves people are just busy. Or we may tell ourselves we don't care, thus minimizing the importance the person has in our life. We may do this with work situations as well, denying that we experienced any loss because we are focused on the new job, career, or business we've started. We are in denial. We refuse to accept that a loss has occurred.

We may become angry at ourselves or others. We may find ourselves blaming others or wanting to hold others accountable if we are angry at them for the loss they caused us or the perception that they caused the loss.

Often there's a tendency to misdirect our emotion, finding it easier to express anger at people who aren't the true source of our anger, such as family members or close friends. Or we may find it easier to express our anger at people we aren't as reliant on for our emotional wellbeing, including store clerks, slow baristas or waiters, and public servants.

Whereas healthy anger is important, unhealthy anger is detrimental and can even be dangerous, not only to our health but also to the safety and wellbeing of others. Wanting revenge is a sign of unhealthy anger. Revenge could include a desire to physically harm someone or their property, destroy the person's relationships with others, damage the individual's career or reputation, and the like.

I need to emphasize that the desire for revenge is very likely a cry for professional help. No matter how hurt you feel, choosing revenge or doing things to harm another person is a destructive course. A healthy choice in this situation is for you to get the support you need to process your emotions, so you can move forward with your life.

If a crime has been committed, you have every right to report it and seek justice—and your emotions are valid. But you also need to be able to manage what's happening internally, so the anger doesn't implode and do damage.

The healthy way to address anger is to be present with it—to sit with it. We neither deny it, stuff it, nor vent it. Instead, we allow ourselves to *feel* it. When we allow our anger to arise, but we don't act it out—don't vent it on someone—the energy trapped in our rage is gradually integrated into our being. Instead of being stuck in a state of frozen rage, this energy becomes available for us to reinvest it in our ongoing journey.

Anger is a tough one in our society. Some people are reactive, exploding and acting out their anger. Others stuff and suppress it. For a period of time, in therapeutic circles, it was believed that "venting" anger was healthy.

Science writer Daniel Goleman, in his outstanding book *Emotional Maturity*, suggests that it is unhealthy to think of our anger in terms of a volcano that needs to blow its top in order to bring us relief. He suggests that the endorsement of venting as a coping skill is counterproductive, and leads to the habit of exploding negative energy and words onto others. Goleman recommends that we allow ourselves to feel the angry feelings, breathing deeply and moving through them. Instead of acting out our anger, which is like exercising a muscle, thus making it bigger, we could quietly observe and feel our angry feelings, until they dissipate of their own accord.

Whenever anger arises, if at all possible find a quiet place and allow yourself to watch the anger you are feeling without becoming caught up in it. Don't suppress it, but don't vent it either—just feel it. *Feeling an emotion is fundamentally different from acting it out.*

What If Scenarios

"If only . . ." mental scenarios may begin to disrupt us, such as, "If they had only given me the raise I asked for, I would have stayed with the company." Or "If only he had gone to counseling, we might have been able to work things out."

These scenarios may take the form of *what ifs*. We may mentally create all kinds of alternative realities that might have been. We have a tendency to do this when things happen in our life that are out of our control. "What if" scenarios are ways we can avoid feeling the impact a loss. I've seen clients do this with regard to divorce, especially when they were the one leaving the marriage. "If only he hadn't cheated," someone says. "If only she drank less," another opines. "Maybe if I'd been more understanding," we tell ourselves. Or we reflect, "Perhaps I was too selfish." We come up with multiple alternative realities to prevent actual reality from settling in, which would require us to face the truth of our loss.

Once we cease creating multiple mental scenarios in which things turn out differently, we may begin feeling sad or even depressed about the changes that have taken place in our lives. It's best to feel our feelings, then feel our feelings some more, even if we fear our tears will ever end.

To make sense of what's happening to us, it helps to realize that expansion is always followed by contraction. We've made big changes by stepping outside of our comfort zone, so there's an automatic tendency to contract. The bigger our expansion, the greater the possibility that we'll scare ourselves and experience an urge to cocoon. It's important to accept the sadness we feel as a perfectly normal response and not tell ourselves something is wrong. Life can feel extremely flat during this period, with a loss of interest in most, if not all, of the activities that usually excite and engage us.

You'll need to assess whether or not the degree of sadness you experience in this stage warrants professional assistance. If it does, don't wait. Seek help. If you begin to think of harming yourself, or feel you'd be better off dead, are unable to get out of bed, or have lost interest in life, get professional support.

If you feel sad to the point of being depressed, you haven't failed. It does not mean you made a mistake in choosing to expand yourself. It means you've become destabilized by the changes you've made in your life. You may need assistance to help you become grounded again. Having the tools to cope effectively is empowering, whereas confusion and overwhelm are paralyzing. Know the warning signs, and know when to get help. You don't need to go it alone. When you have a professional confidante or a support group of likeminded peers moving through their own courageous heart-based evolutions, it eases your transition.

It will take time to integrate all the changes you've made. It will take time to heal from any sense of loss of ourselves in the form of an old way of being, a community, friends, and loved ones, along with perhaps a certain economic status, a home, and/or lifestyle. As we come to accept and *be with* what is now, which requires simply observing it rather than wishing things were different, we begin to feel comfortable with our *new normal*.

Remember, you are growing even when you can't see it. Even as the farmer plants seeds, and they rest in the darkness before springing to life and breaking through the soil into the light, so it is with your own growth. Don't dig up your seeds to examine how they are doing. You've planted your dreams, and you need to allow them time to develop and ripen. Trust the process and allow the seeds to break through the darkness into the light on their own schedule. Before long, you'll see the results and celebrate the milestones of living an authentic, self-authored life.

INVITATION

Write a letter to yourself that you'll open a year from today. Begin the letter by acknowledging yourself for the courageous steps you've taken on your journey of an authentic life of fulfillment. Write it as if the dreams you hearticulated have already come true. Acknowledge your personal qualities, as well as the internal resources you've mustered, to get you to this place today. Write about how delighted you are with yourself for staying on the journey, keeping your heart open, hearticulating and pursuing your dreams.

When you're done, put the letter in an envelope and write the date of one year from now on it. Seal the envelope and put it someplace where you'll remember to open it exactly a year from now. Don't open it sooner.

Not every part of your dream is going to be in place by this time next year. However, you can trust that there is a friendly universe working on your behalf to bring you perfect fulfillment as long as you keep living from your heart and letting life, not your head, lead.

Part Four

Be the Author of Your Life

CHAPTER NINETEEN

Turn Your Heart's Desires into Gold

"All of our dreams can come true if we have the courage to pursue them."
—*Walt Disney*

An alchemist referred to someone who, during the Middle Ages, attempted to transform base metals into gold. The practice, *alchemy*, eventually developed into the modern science of chemistry. Alchemy was widely practiced by philosophers for over four centuries in Egypt, China, India, Greece, and Europe. In time, alchemy came to symbolize the transformation of human character.

Many spiritual teachers have suggested that the practice of alchemy was never really about actually turning lead into gold; rather it was concerned with transforming our minds and becoming enlightened. Carl Jung also suggested that alchemy was about personal transformation.[1]

Thus, Paulo Coelho writes in his novel *The Alchemist:*

"This is why alchemy exists," the boy said. "So that everyone will search for his treasure, find it, and then want to be better than he was in his former life. Lead will play its role until the world has no further need for lead; and then lead will have to turn itself into gold. That's what alchemists do. They show that, when we strive to become better than we are, everything around us becomes better, too."[2]

I believe when you choose to live from love, rather than ego, and follow your inner compass, you're transforming yourself from lead to gold. I also believe that you can create financial alchemy in your life when you transform what you love doing into some or all of your livelihood. Of course, this requires business knowhow as well.

If you so desire, in the pages that follow, you will learn an alchemical formula for turning your heart's desires into gold.

Seduce Your Muse

In 2006, I spent three weeks in Venice, Italy, on a personal writing retreat. I found that being in a place overflowing with Renaissance art, beautiful architecture, and music inspired my creative spirit. Working in a prison with its rigidity and structure had impacted my own spontaneity. I needed to feel free. I wanted to connect with my heart again and give my frontal lobes a break.

My personal writing retreat allowed me to listen to my authentic calling, enjoy time alone, feel freedom, connect with my creativity, and enjoy the beauty of Italy. Traveling allowed me to feel spacious, to explore and have adventures. I enjoyed the experience so much, I wanted to share it with other writers and messengers.

In 2011, I rented two beautiful flats in an Italian Palazzo alongside a canal and created a writing workshop that combined creativity coaching, writing coaching, and breakthrough life coaching. I invited writers and people who wanted to write a book to join me for this retreat so they could transform their lives. My aim was to help them break through their blocks and create more beautiful, compelling pieces. I also invited healers and messengers who didn't identify themselves as writers and yet had empowering messages to share.

I had more responsibilities to my guests as their host: attending to their creature comforts, supporting them in tapping into their creativity and connecting with their voices. However, watching them connect to the sheer bliss of being alive in a vibrant new environment added something wonderful to my experience. It felt good. I came alive in new ways as I attended to the details of the retreat, planning every day's writing goals, special outings, and rituals. Playing host allowed me to connect with the right hemisphere of my brain, which was underutilized in my daily grind at the prison. Thinking outside of the box, focusing on bringing writers out of their heads and into their hearts brought me deep satisfaction.

Everyone who attended the Seduce Your Muse writing retreat told me that they walked away with a deeper sense of self, great new writing pieces, and felt more connected to their authentic selves. They awakened, and that brought me joy! I knew I was doing the real work that I was here to do: to help people connect with their hearts. It took courage for them to invest their time and resources and to leave their routines to travel across the world for a writing retreat. It took audacity for me to hold space for the participants and create an opportunity that would support each one's growth—deep transformation, not just surface-level stuff—while bringing them joy. When it worked, it was amazing!

How did I do this? I got clear on what my heart was calling for and what makes me come alive: beauty, freedom, creativity, connection, travel, helping bring out the best in others, and helping others connect with authenticity and courage, so they could cut through life's bullshit to what really matters. I wanted to support people in having a fully self-expressed, authentic life. That's my commitment, helping people to bring out their best selves.

I combined the elements of what I loved.

1. Travel
2. Writing
3. Beauty
4. Coaching

I made a plan. I located a place to host the retreat, created the curriculum, and got busy on designing the most transformational writing and personal growth retreat I could imagine. More than a retreat, a memorable lifetime experience.

On the metaphysical level, I invited the Universe, through affirmative prayer, to bring together the perfect combination of individuals for this alchemical encounter.

On the physical level, I put the word out and asked others to support my endeavors by sharing word of the retreat. I made my own travel plans, booked the place, and got busy letting people know what I was doing. I put skin in the game.

Many of the people I thought would join me didn't. But I didn't give up. It was getting down to the wire, however, a few weeks before I was to board my plane to Italy, I booked the last spot.

This first retreat was absolutely life changing for me. It was a moment in time when every aspect of my life lined up. It created powerful transformation in my own life and since then I've led four more such retreats in Italy.

Doing what I love has brought me enormous joy and has expanded my understanding of what's possible. I live my dreams not only for myself, but in service of others. This is my personal alchemical formula.

The Traveling Musician's Alchemy

Matthew S. Donowick knew as a young boy that his heart's calling was to play music. He began playing the saxophone when he was twelve, and his parents supported his musical interests by buying him a drum set. When he was twenty-two, this Ohio boy packed up a duffle bag and his guitar, then headed west to the Golden State. He found himself in

Mendocino, a coastal city in northern California known for its redwood forests, organic farms, liberal politics, and local artists. Matthew finally felt at home. He loved nature and was deeply passionate about the preservation of earth and the importance of community.

In his new environment, he thrived! Matthew changed his surname to Human. Human dedicated himself to music and sustainable living. This is what made him come alive! He believed that if he prioritized eating organic food, regardless of cost, the Earth would find a way to support him.

Human began writing songs about his love of nature. He also reached out to his local community and asked them to support him in making an album and music videos for his song. He was met with great support and when he released his album it was deemed word of mouth-worthy and his listenership grew.

After he wrote the 2006 song "Don't Blame Me, I Voted for Willie Nelson," Human found himself opening for Willie at one of his concerts.[3]Human now tours in a biodiesel vehicle and sings at farmers' markets across the country.

Human follows his heart to great success, turning what he loves into gold. He's produced seven albums, five music festivals, and hundreds of shows. He plays guitar, piano, saxophone, harmonica, and is studying the banjo. Because he chooses to play his music in more backwoods locations (an important part of his alchemical formula), rather than major cities, he enjoys great freedom and his life is vibrant, rich with connections, travel, and natural beauty. His music was recently featured in the documentary *Occupy Love*.[4]

The Alchemy of Beer and Pizza

Mike and Brian, two brothers who loved drinking beer, invented a special Ruby Ale, which derived its pinkish hue from adding raspberries to the hops they brewed. It was 1985 and they were the first brewers in the United States to legally use fruit in the brewing process.

The brothers, who loved drinking beer, eating pizza, and watching movies, thought it would be cool to open a movie theater where the patrons enjoy their Ruby Ale while eating pizza in a movie theater. Two years later, they bought a historic church building in Northwest Portland and converted it into a theater which they named the Mission. It was a huge hit.

The McMenamin brothers were following their hearts and doing what they loved, and they were met with huge success in brewing ale, selling beer and pizza, and creating a thriving pub community.

Continuing with their alchemical formula of combining what they loved, they bought more buildings, specifically historic landmarks in Oregon and Washington State. The brothers were passionate about creating environments where people could come together in community, like the pubs of Europe where people gathered. By turning these buildings into friendly gathering places that served beer, pizza, and other good pub food, they were preserving the history and architecture of Pacific Northwest cities and creating opportunities for their fellow Oregonians to enjoy the treasures of the region.

I remember when they bought the rundown Bagdad movie theater, a place I watched movies at when I was a kid. Hawthorne Street in Portland, where the theater was located, was always cool. After the McMenamin brothers refurbished the Bagdad and converted it into a theater pub where you could watch a movie while eating pizza and drinking beer or soda, relaxing on the sofas with your feet on the table, it brought new life to the neighborhood. I'm sure it raised property values. When you turn what you love into gold, it lifts everyone around you.

I think the McMenamin's most exciting "adventure-prise," as Ernest Chu, author of *Soul Currency,* would call it, was when they bought the seventy-four-acre complex that was once the Multnomah County Poor House in Troutdale, Oregon. The Edgefield Manor, as it later became known, had housed the poor, the sick, and the elderly. During the Great Depression, 614 people lived at the Edgefield. In the 1960s and 1970s, it housed institutionalized emotionally disturbed children.

I remember driving by the creepy old place when I was kid. When I was twelve, they shut it down and were going to demolish it. Then someone who loved history and old buildings stepped in to prevent its destruction. In 1990, the McMenamin brothers purchased the place and put Troutdale on the map. The Edgefield, as it's known today, is no longer creepy but beautiful. It has a hotel with a hundred European-style guest rooms and hostel accommodations, a brewpub, a gourmet restaurant, a movie theater, a full spa, an artisan area replete with glass blowers and potters, an organic garden, a distillery, and a winery.[5] The place is a grownup kid's playground.

The brothers have continued to use this winning formula of purchasing historic buildings and creating places where people can gather as a community and have fun. The McMenamins' empire has grown to over sixty-six establishments, including pubs, historic hotels, theater pubs, breweries, and music venues. Nine of their buildings are on the National Register of Historic Buildings.

Turtle Time Alchemy

In her early twenties, Carmen Goodyear felt her calling to go to the countryside and learn how to be self-sufficient. It was the 1970s, a time when a women's back to the land movement was a foot. Carmen traveled to Northern California and bought an old farm in Mendocino County. Carmen lived in a tiny twelve-by-twelve-foot pump house that fit only a bed, a couple of bookshelves, and a wood stove. This was her Walden Pond.

Being in nature, creating art, gardening, learning new things, and being self-sufficient all made Carmen come alive. She felt a deep sense of peace. These were her alchemical elements.

She also had support. Several women bought land in the surrounding area. A group known as the Seven Sisters Construction Company, a thriving women's construction company from Berkeley, California, came and built a beautiful octagonal barn on Carmen's property.

During the twenty-eight years she lived in this tiny cabin. She learned how to be self-sufficient, developing skills in construction, plumbing, animal husbandry, and gardening. She bought a few goats and chickens, planted a vegetable patch, and lived off the land and the goat's milk and goat cheese she made. Carmen lived harmoniously with nature.

She also had a passion for painting and wanted to paint the world around her. She attended a women's painting group where she met Laurie York. They two became friends. Eventually, they began painting together, and fell in love. They shared a passion for animals, nature, painting, photography, and filmmaking. A year later they moved in together, or more accurately, Laurie moved into another cabin on the land. Together they named the farm Turtle Time Farm. They wanted a slower pace of life that they called *turtle time*.

They created multiple streams of income selling organic vegetables, goat cheese that Carmen made from the goat's milk, and eggs from the chickens. The eggs were so delicious and healthy that one of the most well-known restauranteurs in the Napa Valley began ordering them on a regular basis and paying top dollar.

When Carmen was in her fifties, a Redwood tree on her property fell during a storm. She designed and built a new one-room cabin with the wood. She installed a new stove, which she used for heating and cooking, and this time installed a shower. She still uses the outhouse, because honestly, sitting on it is one of the highlights of the day. It has a great view!

In 2000, Carmen and Laurie also invested in their first computer and video camera. After making a series of short films, the couple decided to make a feature-length film about marriage equality for same-sex couples. Laurie had contacted me about a marriage equality rally I was organizing in Sacramento on Valentine's Day 2004 that included comedian Margaret Cho and Reverend Troy Perry, who founded the world's first gay and lesbian church, the Metropolitan Community Church.

Two days before the rally, on February 12, 2004, San Francisco Mayor Gavin Newsom lifted the ban on same-sex marriage, and San Francisco City Hall began marrying same-sex couples. That night Carmen and Laurie jumped in their car and drove to San Francisco. The next morning, they filmed couples getting married and tied the knot themselves. Then they drove to Sacramento and filmed the marriage equality rally that was enthusiastically attended by newlyweds and invigorated supporters. After the rally, they drove back to their farm and began working on their documentary.

Freedom to Marry: The Journey to Justice documentary, created by rural goat farmers and released in 2005, became one of the world's most watched films on marriage equality. It was picked up by PBS and shown at LGBT film festivals and other film festivals around the world. The documentary was translated into four languages (Spanish, French, Chinese, and Dutch) and was screened and won awards in San Francisco, Los Angeles, Portland, Austin,

Tucson, Atlanta, Berlin, Brussels, Madrid, Buenos Aires, Barcelona, Australia, and Taiwan.

The couple went on to found Mendocino Coast Films and made several more amazing documentaries, including their most recent film, *Women on the Land: Creating Conscious Community*, about the 1970s women's back to the land movement.

Carmen and Laurie's journey is another example of how alchemy can work even for goat farmers in rural Mendocino. Following their hearts allowed them to make a positive difference on a global level and they were able to support others in following their hearts too. In 2018, they celebrated twenty-four years together.

An Alchemical Path to Wellness

Andrea had a dream of running her own eastern-style wellness center. Andrea knew it was her calling to be an acupuncturist. She loved helping people and loved eastern medicine. She was working as an acupuncturist at a clinic and running the business for the absentee owner who'd built the business twenty-five years earlier. The business was starting to slow down, and Andrea could see that it needed revitalization. She was excited to offer him ideas to upgrade the business, but the owner was resistant to her suggestions. She wanted to work in a place that was more relaxed and cooperative, more like a spa environment than a doctor's office. She imagined a place that was different than traditional Chinese medicine clinics.

Andrea began to dream of creating her own wellness center and offering more than acupuncture. Andrea took a part-time job at a spa that emulated the kind of environment and approach she was looking for. She consulted with the spa's owner and learned from her how to run a business from a collaborative model. Over time, Andrea's confidence grew. A few years later, when the doctor decided to sell his practice, Andrea bought it.

The last time I saw Andrea, she was showing me around her new wellness center. She'd given the place quite a makeover. The rooms were warm and inviting. They no longer looked like dental offices or rooms with hospital beds. Andrea, who'd appeared quite tentative and passive when I first met her, was confident and excited about her new business. Getting support and collaborating with others is an important part of the alchemical recipe.

Cross-Continental Alchemy

I met Cory, an intern I supervised during my years as a prison psychologist, more than a decade since he and his family had fled Kenya. When he was a teen, his parents were journalists who advocated for a multiparty system a precursor to a democratic system—because there was a one-party system, like a dictatorship, and the president and his government didn't appreciate these other voices. Dissenters, including Cory's parents, faced ongoing threats, imprisonments, bombings, and death threats. The family came to the United States seeking asylum.

Cory loved cycling and hiking and was interested in health psychology. After completing his internship, he took a job working with obese children and began training for triathlons. In no time at all, he was placing at the top in competitions. He decided to create family triathlons and fitness days because he loved bringing together fitness and psychology. He was doing what he loved, positively impacting the children's lives and his practice was thriving.

Cory missed the land of his childhood, but because his application for U.S. citizenship still hadn't been approved, he was unable to travel outside the States. When he was finally granted citizenship, he and his spouse planned a long-awaited journey back to Kenya. When he returned we met for coffee and he shared with me how he wanted to take runners to Kenya, just like I took writers to Italy.

Cory wanted to share the beauty of his Kenya with Americans. He envisioned seasoned runners, marathoners, and even first-timers enjoying the athletic experience of a lifetime running with the Kenyans. "People travel to Boston and New York to run," he told me, "so why shouldn't they run with the people known for being the best runners on the planet?" He wanted people to have an opportunity to run on the plains of Africa, go on safari, visit the bustling city of Nairobi, and to have an authentic experience of Kenya and engage with its rich culture and variety of Kenya's diverse people (there are over forty-three different tribes and over sixty-eight different languages spoken in Kenya).

Cory found the unique alchemical formula that would turn his passion into gold as he authored his own authentic career. In addition to his successful private practice, he leads an annual Run Like a Kenyan—In Kenya excursion where participants get to run, eat, sleep, and live like a Kenyan because they stay with Cory's extended family in their homes (for details see RuninKenya.com).

INVITATION
Creating Your Alchemical Formula

Combine the ingredients of what you love to find the special alchemical formula with which to generate gold in your own life.

Step 1. Identify your heart's calling. Each of us brings our unique set of gifts, talents, interests, hobbies, and experiences to the table. When we paint the canvas of our lives from our diverse palette, we create our own masterpieces. We design a life that works for us.

Step 2. Get clear on what makes you come alive. The second step in the alchemical formula is to get clear on what brings vitality into your life. What do you love to do? What makes you come alive? What brings joy into your life? Where are you most contented? In what kind of environment do you thrive? If you could choose how you spent each day, what would you be doing most days?

Step 3. Combine the elements of what you love. In this alchemical process, you want to bring together two to four elements you love to create your golden formula for success.

Step 4. Get support. To turn what you love into gold, it's best to get a mentor whose doing what you love or can support you in doing what you love. Getting support from others creates synergy and is an important step in your success formula.

Step 5. Take action. The final step of creating your alchemical success formula is to take specific actions on your dreams and heart's desires. Remember, without pairing hearticulation with action, you are only dreaming.

As you reflect on your heart's calling and what makes you come alive and begin to explore combining those elements together, you'll likely feel invigorated and excited about the possibilities of creating your alchemical gold.

At the same time, you might find it a little scary. It may even feel like you're waking a sleeping dragon inside you. You will be drawn out of your comfort zone, that means you're growing. The alternative of growing, keeping yourself busy and ignoring your heart's desire, will prove pretty uncomfortable in the long run. There is satisfaction in following your heart. So, I invite you to follow your heart and be an alchemist!

CHAPTER TWENTY

Don't Get Bitter,
Make It Better

"Make each day your masterpiece."
—John Wooden

Marcos Apolonio was a Seventh Day Adventist minister in Sao Paulo, Brazil, for the largest congregation in South America. The church had 3,500 members. Married with children, Pastor Marcos, had lived with a secret since he was a boy. He was gay. He'd known since he was five years old. However, growing up in a Latino country in a religion that viewed same-sex love as a sin, he knew that he would be considered a sinner. He went to a minister when he was fifteen and asked him if the feelings would go away. The minister gave him no hope.

Marcos went deep into the closet. He prayed to God to change his thoughts and feelings. When that failed, he devoted his life to God and the Adventist church. He became a pastor. He taught bible classes. He gave sermons.

He married a woman. He had children. While he respected and loved his wife, and cherished his children, nothing could override the fact that he was gay.

Marcos secretly went to therapy to resolve what he believed was causing his homosexuality. He hid his therapy because he said therapy is seen as suspect by conservative church members "because they believe that all you need is Jesus. They view therapy as a sign of weakness."[1] The therapist employed conversion therapy techniques, rather than helping Marcos love and accept himself. One therapist told Marcos that eating garlic would help him release his same-sex feelings. He ate a ton of garlic. Needless to say, it didn't change anything. He did say that therapy helped him learn some coping skills so it wasn't a total waste of money.

I interviewed Marcos for my audio program *How to Come Out of the Closet and Into Your Power.* He shared how in his desperation he got romantically involved with a man he met on the internet whom he later discovered was jealous and disturbed. When Marcos tried to end the relationship, the man threatened to "out" him to the church officials. The man started stalking him and his family. He told Marcos, "I'm going to ruin your life."

Rather than having her hear the truth from the disgruntled ex-lover, Marcos went to his wife and told her that he was gay. He apologized to her for living a lie. The man went to the church officials and showed them email correspondence between him and Marcos, outing Marcos as gay. The church officials called Marcos in for a meeting to question him. When Marcos told them it was true, he'd had a relationship with a man, they fired him on the spot.

Devastated by the loss of his job, his community of friends, and the abrupt ending of his married life, Marcos decided to go to the United States. When he arrived he felt "broken." He said, "I had nobody. I was completely alone. I lost literally everything." And when he arrived in the United States he said he found out that "the air company lost my luggage. I lost one hundred percent. Everything. But I didn't lose God."

Marcos, grateful that he still had his relationship with God, said, "Suffering can make you bitter or it can make you better. We have to decide."

Marcos got work in construction and then as a janitor so he could support himself and send money for his children. He continued to seek church conversion therapy. It still didn't work. He then reached out to a Seventh Day Adventist program called Kinship that helps LGBT people who've been kicked out of the church. This is where his healing began. He found other pastors, pastor's wives, teachers, social workers, psychologists, straight people, and LGBT people who were all working together to change the church's policy condemning LGBT people. It was there that he met the man to whom he's now married.

Rather than giving up or becoming bitter, Marcos has overcome his circumstances and has made his life better. Today he is a licensed social worker living in California with his husband. He is a part of the leadership of a world-wide ministry of LGBT and heterosexual Seventh Day Adventists who are working to change the church's stance on LGBT people. He is ministering to an international population and helping other people make their lives better. He is grateful to say, "Today, I have nothing to hide." He said that he lost a lot of friends, but those who are in his life now are closer to him than they ever were before. Now he knows his friends are genuine friends and that he is loved for exactly who he is, his authentic self, not for the man he was pretending to be.

Pastor Marcos recognizes that many LGBT people have been harmed by organized religion and shut down their connection with God. He is committed to helping LGBT people get reconnected and stay connected to their spiritual beliefs. He emphasizes that we need to get support and do things that help us get better and make life better.

Spin Your Pain into Goodness

Even experiences that have caused us pain and suffering can help us connect to our authentic essence and by speaking our truth we can turn our pain into opportunities to help others.

As you may recall, actor Christopher Reeve experienced a riding accident that left him a quadriplegic. His misfortune led him to speak out about disabilities and make a difference for himself and other disabled people and their families.

If you are in pain, how might you spin this pain into goodness for yourself and others?

I have worked with several widowed and divorced women in my private practice. Losing a spouse through death or divorce is one of the hardest life experiences. For survivors, not only do you lose the one you loved, you lose a sense of yourself, and your life as you've known it radically changes shape. Finding your footing after a huge transition, such as a divorce, can be extremely challenging.

Angela hired me after the death of her husband. She was looking for meaning and direction in her life after the loss of a twenty-year marriage. Prior to her marriage she'd loved performing. However, it had been years since she'd been on the stage. Even her work, as an insurance agent, kept her behind the scenes. Now she felt it was time to reclaim this part of her authentic essence, the part that wanted to be more fully self-expressed. Angela chose to channel her pain into expressive movement and poetry to express the grief and overwhelm she felt following her husband's sudden death. It was so meaningful to her to reengage this part of herself that she ended up creating a powerful theatrical performance that she performed on stage in her local theater. Angela was happy that she had found a way to turn her pain into something creative that she could share with others and that ultimately led to a deeper understanding of her experience as a widow.

Another client, Kristina, came to me after receiving a medical diagnosis. She wanted to regain her health and help other women who struggle with weight gain. Kristina combined health and fitness activities with her passion for writing to create a business that focused on women's health, wellness, positive body image, and self-love. Kristina designed writing workshops that focused on body issues and served healthy food. She wrote articles about health and nutrition and began working as a personal trainer to assist women in meeting their fitness goals.

Two of my clients, Irene and Cassie, had experienced childhood abuse and struggled with substance abuse since they were teenagers. Both of these women lost many good years of their lives making poor decisions that entangled them in bad relationships and landed them in correctional facilities for a period of time. Each of these women sought treatment for their childhood abuse and addiction. After getting clean and sober, each individually had decided to pursue a degree, one in mental health and the other in drug and alcohol counseling. Today, they are both helping other men and women with addictions recover. Each woman found a way to turn her personal challenges into a chance to improve the lives of others.

Another client of mine, Pamela, lost her child to a drunk driver. After many years of therapy to help her cope with the terrible death of her daughter, she began speaking out about the dangers of drunk driving. She took her painful loss and used it to help educate others to help reduce drunk driving. Her actions could not bring back her child, but she found that it helped her to know that she was doing something to prevent other people's children from being killed by people who made the mistake of driving under the influence.

Many nonprofit organizations that exist today were started by mothers whose children were hurt or killed and wanted to make a difference to help other parents protect their children, such as Mothers Against Drunk Driving (MADD), Parents and Friends of Lesbians and Gays

(PFLAG), and Parents of Murdered Children (POMC). These are all examples of people taking their pain and using it to help others.

A Sage Survivor

You've heard the expression *sage advice*. Being *sage* means you have acquired the kind of wisdom as a result of reflecting on your experiences. It implies the use of prudence and good judgment.

Drawing on wisdom gained from her experience as a survivor of childhood human sex trafficking and adult prostitution, Norma Hotaling was able to offer sage advice to other prostitutes, helping them get off drugs and off the streets. Her aim was to educate *johns,* the slang term for the clients of prostitutes, to the dangers of sex for hire, holding them and pimps accountable for sex crimes against minors. Working her alchemy in this way, she was able to bring national attention to the issue of the sexual exploitation of women and children.

In 1992, Norma founded the SAGE Project (an acronym for standing against global exploitation). SAGE's mission is to "provide a safe place for survivors to leave lives of sexual exploitation, addiction, and trauma."[2] Norma's intent was for survivors to begin living safe, healthy lives free of coercion and abuse. SAGE has one of the longest running john schools, diversion programs for men who solicit prostitutes, in the country.

Norma was able to do much to help make the world a better place. Although she passed away in 2008, the SAGE Project continues to help survivors leave the streets and the drugs behind them, going on to live productive and fulfilling lives. The program is run by graduates of the project who help other survivors and work in partnership with the San Francisco Police Department and the District Attorney's Office to help police and politicians understand the dynamics of trauma and exploitation.

Marcos, Angela, Norma, Kristina, Irene, Cassie, and Pamela are living examples of how to take life's "lemons" and make lemonade. Each one of them found a way to turn life's struggles and hardships into a platform from which to help others. We too have a choice to make. We can choose to let the negative circumstances in our lives drag us down or we can find a way to help ourselves and help others in the process.

INVITATION

Take some time to reflect on the challenges in your own life. Identify the sources of pain or experiences that caused you hardship and begin to imagine how you could spin those negative experiences into opportunities to help others. Is there an organization out there doing something that you could join and help make a difference? What are some productive ways you could use your loss, sadness, or pain to motivate you to take action or make choices that would channel that pain into something good for you and others?

CHAPTER TWENTY-ONE

Set Boundaries

"The formula is simple: In any given situation, detach and ask, "What do I need to do to take care of myself?"
—Melody Beattie

On the road to living an authentic life in hot pursuit of our dreams, we need to stay focused on our lives. When we start doing for others what they need to do for themselves we're no longer focused on doing for ourselves what no one else can do for us. Setting boundaries is critical if we want to create our own fulfilling lives. If we waste energy enabling others, we've abandoned our dreams. It's just like if you're bowling and you take your ball and use your turn to help the other person in the lane next to yours knock down their pins. If you do, you're no longer focusing on what's happening in the game. You're not playing in your own lane.

Many of us have been taught to put the needs of others before our own. In fact, this is the expectation for women in many cultures. We may have been taught this by witnessing the selflessness of a parent or having grown up with religious teaching that admonished us not to be "selfish," instead advocating selflessness, even martyrdom.

Setting limits and boundaries is about focusing on what we need to do to care for ourselves and not doing for others what they can and should be doing for themselves. It's not that we don't help others, but we don't engage in helping that hurts us. That's the definition of *codependency*.

In her book *Codependent No More*, recovery expert Melody Beattie writes, "We rescue people from their responsibilities. We take care of people's responsibilities for them. Later we get mad at *them* for what *we've* done. Then we feel used and sorry for ourselves. That is the pattern, the triangle."[1] She describes a codependent person as "one who has let another person's behavior affect him or her, and who is obsessed with controlling that person's behavior."[2]

How do we keep our eyes on our own lane and not get caught up in the drama of the lives of others? How do we stop controlling or being affected? We set limits.

Perhaps you have friends or family members who are constantly in crisis. You can send them loving energy, hold them in your prayers, and set aside some time to support them if you see fit. Don't let yourself get sucked in to listening to the same old stories, especially if they aren't willing to get help or do anything to change their circumstances. If sharing with a friend becomes asymmetrical, one of you needs to schedule a therapy or coaching session.

And establishing boundaries is about more than just setting limits. Boundaries are about self-care. When we set limits at work or with friends and family members, we keep ourselves from becoming overloaded, overscheduled, overcommitted, and thus, overwhelmed. This is important for our physical and mental health and emotional stability. If we're spinning too many plates in the air, it's just a matter of time before they all come crashing down. Boundaries get us to pay attention to what our limits are and then set them accordingly.

We need to say no to requests sometimes. We need to be able to bring up our concerns. We need to be able to take time for ourselves when we feel depleted. To truly honor your authentic self, you need to bring up concerns, speak your truth, and do what you're feeling called to do, even if that means disappointing others, changing plans, or putting up your do not disturb sign so you can connect back with yourself.

The biggest reason we don't take time for ourselves and say no is guilt. We believe others will think we are being selfish. Maybe we even believe that we are being selfish. However, if someone sincerely cares for you, that person is going to want you to do what's best for you. If you find that you have a pattern of not showing up for the people around you ever, that's another story. Perhaps if that's the case for you, you are selfish. However, if you need to say no because you need that time for self-restoration or to invest in your dreams and the things that will not take root if you don't make time for them, then the people who really value you will respect your no.

I truly believe that when you do something that is right for you, it's ultimately the best thing for others too. Let's say you know a relationship isn't working out, but you're afraid to end it because you don't want to hurt the other person. I see this with my clients a lot. They're unhappy, but they're afraid to break things off.

It's only when we are true to ourselves that we can be of any real value to another. If we are denying some part of ourselves or our truth, we will ultimately fail to be a source of joy for ourselves and for anyone else.

A coworker of mine in the federal prison always said. "Boundaries are our friends." They keep us safe, like guardrails or lines on the highway, they show us where we are safe to be and where we are in danger. Personal boundaries designate clear limits. They allow us and others to know what is okay and what is not. They help us know what we are okay with and what we are not okay with. They let us know where we begin and end and what is ours and what is another's. Whether it is physical space, personal possessions, ways of communicating, thoughts, or opinions, boundaries outline what is ours.

Boundaries allow us to connect with our truth. When we know our boundaries, we are able to speak up for ourselves and ask for what we need. Boundaries are about knowing our own edges. Boundaries allow us to know when someone or something is taking us not just out of the comfort zone of our ego, but out of our essence—causing us to go against ourselves. Knowing and setting our personal boundaries keeps us from abandoning our truth.

The Cost of People Pleasing

Sometimes we do things that go against ourselves to please others or because we are afraid of losing love and approval. However, when we do this we are being unloving to ourselves. By doing things that are against our own essence, we will ultimately lose our own approval.

In relationships of any kind, take a look at your behaviors. Do you do things to please others? When someone asks you what you'd like to do, do you find yourself replying in one of the following ways?

- "I don't know."
- "Whatever you'd like to do."
- "You decide."

There are times when we might honestly be happy to let someone else lead. However, when we defer to another to please them, we are denying our real preferences and beginning to settle for a life that is less satisfying. If we stop doing the things we love, we will become disconnected from ourselves and resentful of the people we have prioritized ahead of us. Staying in touch with *your* heart's desires, not just those of your spouse, partner, or friends, is of paramount importance in your ongoing journey.

Following your heart is about being willing to do the things you love even when those you are close to don't wish to. Choosing to spend time following your own bliss comes with its own rewards, so don't underestimate the importance of making time for *you*.

For example, Mark loved the outdoors. He enjoyed surfing, kayaking, hiking, and cycling. The grounding he received from nature helped him navigate the challenges that came up for him in his demanding work as an attorney. Unfortunately, he had a habit of getting into long-term relationships with women who didn't share his passion for the outdoors. The women he chose typically preferred lazy weekends that included sleeping in, brunch, and shopping.

Because Mark had a tendency to put his partner's interests ahead of his own, he found he was becoming disconnected from himself. To counter this, I gave him a homework assignment of scheduling two dates a month when he was to do the things he loved to do—surf, hike, kayak, bike. This was an important way for him to stay connected to his own heart's desires, which ultimately made him a better partner both at the law firm and for his significant other, since he was more solid in himself, happier, and more relaxed.

Don't do things just to please others. Do things because you want to grow or try something new. Make your actions conscious choices. If you compromise, do it because you want to see where it takes you. However, think long and hard before you do something that is not good for you. Be clear that when you do something that goes against your boundaries you will likely end up resenting the other person and may ultimately lose your self-respect.

For example, let's say your lover wants to engage in a new sexual behavior. You agree to try it out because you're open to the exploration and seeing if it's something you might enjoy. You willingly participate with your love in this new adventure. But in doing so, you realize it's not your thing. You don't enjoy it. You've come to the edge of yourself and you know what you like and don't like with regard to this aspect of intimacy. You tell your partner, "I'm glad we tried that and I'm not interested in doing that again." Your partner, on the other hand, really enjoyed it. A few days later your partner asks you to do it again, despite the fact that you've shared your truth with him/her. If you choose to do it again because you feel like maybe it was just a fluke, then you are choosing it and that's not people pleasing.

If you engage in the behavior again to please your partner or not to lose his or her love, you are now going against yourself. You are not respecting your boundaries and you are allowing your lover to disregard your boundaries as well. If you continue to do this, you have abandoned or even betrayed yourself.

This is not just in the area of sexual intimacy, but other behaviors. For example, my client Mei-ling, an interior designer, gave up her job when she married. Her husband, Ray, was in law school when they were dating and after they married he took his first job with a firm that had hefty time requirements. With his need to rack up billable hours, plus his ambition to be on the partner track, Ray was often working twelve-hour days. He also had an unbearable LA commute that was a minimum one hour each way.

Ray had two boys from a previous marriage of whom he had part-time custody. There was no way Ray could take care of his children's needs without hiring a nanny. He made enough money to do so. But instead, he told Mei-ling she could quit her job and he would "take care of her." In return, she agreed to care for the household and the boys during his custody weeks. This made sense to Mei-ling since her business was not off the ground yet.

Mei-ling finished up her obligations to her previous clients and then went about the task of making a home with her husband and stepchildren. A few months into this new arrangement, she found that Ray, a generous boyfriend, was quite tight with the purse strings as a husband. He deposited all his paychecks in a private account to which his wife did not have access. He also required her to come up with a budget for everything she needed to run the household. Ray second-guessed her expenditures, especially when it came to spending any money for her own needs, such as clothing, visits to the hair dresser, and so on. Frustrated by this, Mei-ling asked Ray if his paychecks could go into a shared account, so she could have equal access to the money. His angry response surprised her. Ray said she was being "selfish" and "ungrateful." He told her how hard he worked for the money and that "any woman would be lucky to be in her shoes." She questioned herself. "Am I being selfish?"

Mei-ling became very depressed. A few years later, she contacted me. She had a small amount of cash savings from an inheritance, which she used to pay for counseling sessions. She shared with me that she was deeply confused about how she could feel so uncomfortable with her marital situation since her husband was providing for her. She also felt dismayed that she'd let herself become so controlled by a man. She felt small and worthless.

I validated Mei-Ling's feelings and we discussed boundaries. While Mei-ling had agreed to stay home and care for her stepchildren to please her husband, she started to feel that felt her boundaries were being ignored. There was no way her essential self could "get over it." She was losing herself to keep her husband's love.

No matter how many times she tried to find peace with the arrangement and talk herself into being okay with it, her essential self wasn't having it. Things would go well for a while with her husband and then conflicts around money and family responsibilities would resurface and the feelings of goodwill between the two of them would evaporate. Without an income, Mei-ling felt controlled and humiliated by the arrangement.

After several months of our working together, she brought up her concerns with her husband about their arrangement. He became defensive and told her she was completely ungrateful. He even went so far to say that the legal secretaries at his workplace would be happy to be in her shoes.

Hurt and confused by his response, Mei-ling retreated to lick her wounds. A few days later, she had the nagging urge to look in Ray's wallet. When she did, she found receipts to a hotel in Santa Monica. That night she went to check his phone. She told me she felt awful for violating his trust, however something urged her on. She opened messages from his paralegal. The first few were business related, however, as she scrolled on, she started to see texts that were overly familiar and flirtatious. Then she checked the picture mode. It was there that she found the source of what she knew her intuitive nudges were leading her to: infidelity.

Mei-ling said that she'd felt something was going on for a while, but the fact that she didn't have her own income or know what she would do next led to her pull blinders of denial over her eyes. It had been too much. But now, she was ready to deal with the situation head on, eyes wide open. She confronted Ray. He didn't deny his cheating.

Heartbroken, but wiser for the wear, Mei-ling told him she wanted a divorce. He agreed that it would be best.

In my office, Mei-ling asked me what she'd done wrong. I invited her to examine when she began to abandon herself and ignore her boundaries. She realized that it wasn't one thing, but a series of actions she took or failed to take. She had stopped expressing her true opinions and become agreeable to avoid conflict. She had acquiesced to sex when she wasn't in the mood, justifying it as her "wifely duty." Mei-ling had become a role and ceased being a woman. She had let her beliefs and cultural upbringing about what it meant to be a good wife take over.

We can never know how her abandoning herself played into her husband's attraction for the other woman. It is possible that he found his paralegal attractive because she was still being her authentic self to a greater degree than Mei-ling was. Perhaps he still would have cheated. What Mei-ling did know is that she would have felt better about herself if she hadn't allowed her boundaries to be trampled on.

It's critical that you respect your essential self and your boundaries. If you feel angry or depressed about a certain behavior you're engaging in to please others, that's your inner warning system going off. Course correct. Stop and change it. Speak your truth. Find another solution. This is different than being uncomfortable with change. We're all creatures of habit and uncomfortable with change.

But the discomfort associated with growing and stretching by choice is different than the discomfort we feel because we are being stretched thin or stretched in ways that are not right for us. We need to be able to say no and bring up concerns, to speak up, so as not to resent ourselves or others. This is why we need to stay awake, conscious, and connected to our essence so that we know what is right for us. Had Mei-ling stayed connected to herself and listened to her early warning system, she would have realized sooner that the situation was untenable and course corrected so that the balance in her marriage could have been restored or so she and Ray could have charted separate courses.

Our boundaries are ever changing. It's important to take time to listen to and honor our inner wisdom. When we do, we are honoring our authentic selves. Follow your heart, but don't give it away.

INVITATION

Take a look at your relationships. Are there specific people in your life you are caught up in a people-pleasing style of interaction with? What is the cost of that people-pleasing in your life? Do you feel resentful? Are you missing out on other things? Are you engaging in behaviors that are unhealthy to please others? Drinking more than you like to drink? Spending more than you'd like to spend? Ignoring the things that really matter to you?

Now take a look at your calendar. Are there activities or events in your calendar you have agreed to that you are attending out of obligation that are not feeding you? Have you overcommitted yourself to please others?

Give yourself permission to say no to at least one thing you've said yes to that is not in alignment with your authentic essence. If you feel empowered, honestly share with the person or people that you committed to why you're saying no. Additionally, if you're ready to really shake things up and set boundaries let the people in your life know that you are making changes and tell them what you are no longer willing to do and what you plan to do now to make time for yourself and your own healthy wellbeing. You may be surprised to find that setting boundaries for yourself will empower others to be more authentic and share their needs and boundaries on a deeper level.

CHAPTER TWENTY-TWO

Own Your Life

*"Your time is limited, don't waste it living
someone else's life."*
—Steve Jobs

As you've begun to listen to your inner compass and connect more deeply with your essence have you found your life expanding? Perhaps you've felt some nervousness or even experienced a sense of being on a rollercoaster as you've started engaging with life in new ways. At times you may feel a sense of loss that comes with making changes or fears arising to push you backward. Don't worry. Just keep moving forward and allowing yourself to grow. The reminders that follow will support you as you continue to live a life that reflects your passion, dreams, and values.

Stay Present

Slowing down and staying present in your body allows you to remain openhearted. Making time to connect with yourself and clearing mental clutter keeps you in touch with your own thoughts and feelings, which is how you'll know what you truly want for your life. Your ability to hear your own desires is a basic tenet of a fulfilled life.

Are you slowing down and staying present in your body? Are you taking time to clear away the mental clutter? Are you listening to your heart?

Meditation, walks in nature, and keeping a gratitude journal are time-tested practices that will allow you to stay connected to your true self.

Make a Date to Check in with Yourself

When was the last time you wrote in your journal, if you have one? Have you taken yourself out to do something you love just for the fun of it recently? Are you prioritizing what you love in your work and your play? Go to your calendar and make a date with yourself to eat out at your favorite restaurant, take a trip, go for a long drive, or do something else you enjoy. For example, go roller skating, play miniature golf, attend a concert. The important thing is to take time and check in with yourself and your heart's desires.

Surround Yourself with Courageous-Hearted People

Stay committed to bringing people into your life who are living authentic lives themselves. Surround yourself with people who will help you step up your game and increase your willingness to do something new or let something go. Remember the crabs in the barrel story. You don't want to be dragged back down by naysayers. Gather your heart-based tribe members around you—those who are willing to grow, take positive risks, and play a bigger game. Take some time to schedule coffee dates with people who inspire you. If you find it beneficial, get yourself to a Meetup, a meditation group, or a conference of kindred spirits. To mix things up, you may even choose to go to an event or do something you've never done before.

Get Support for Mind, Body, and Spirit

Just as a boxer is supported by a trainer, a coach, and someone to bring them water and massage their shoulders, you need a team on your side. You need people who will help you stay strong, mentally alert, confident, and openhearted. Connect with mentors, healers, guides, and sages you can turn to. A good therapist, life coach, spiritual practitioner, minister, twelve-step sponsor, and so on can be invaluable and support you in building a solid foundation for a life that's healthy and happy. Set up regular checkups with these practitioners, just as you would with your dentist. Most of us get our teeth cleaned every six months. Sometimes we also need a mental clearing of all the negative energy, self-doubt, worry, guilt, and so forth, that has shown up in our lives.

Along with preparing yourself psychically for your journey, nurture your body with massages and energy work. Most of us tend to store emotions in our bodies. A massage, visit to the acupuncturist, or a Reiki session can help free up blocked emotions and give you access to more parts of yourself. Find a massage therapist, acupuncturist, holistic chiropractor, personal trainer, or whatever kind of bodily helper is most suitable for your particular needs. The better you feel physically, the better you'll feel emotionally. The more confident and supported you feel emotionally and psychologically, the more effective you will be at making changes in your life, and the more successful you will be in your new business or career endeavors.

The era of mentally driving ourselves and pushing our bodies at all costs is an old paradigm that has left people disconnected from their hearts, from nature, and from their callings. It's time to move beyond it.

Love Yourself

Engage in practices that are self-nurturing. You will unleash even more of your potential as you embrace the whole of yourself. Forgive yourself for mistakes you made or things you didn't handle as skillfully or ideally as you would have wanted. You will become more authentic as you stop rejecting and loathing parts of yourself. Keep noticing the negative and critical ways you speak to yourself and remember that the critical inner voice is not your true essence. Do what you can to stop or ignore negative self-talk and find ways to speak lovingly to yourself.

Follow Your Heart

Keep following your heart. Check in with yourself and ask, "Where does my heart want to lead me? What are my heart and soul calling me to do?" Your heart and soul's invitations are your very essence speaking to you. Keep moving in the direction of your dreams and remember, following your heart takes bravery. When the head's *shoulds* and *ought tos* arise simply notice them. Ask, "Is this my true self? Is this about other people's ideas and opinions?" Wait for the deep stillness beneath the voice in the head to reveal itself. This is your heart taking the wheel. It is a deep, wordless knowing. Trust it!

Expect Sadness

Just as there will be amazing joys, new opportunities, exciting adventures, and exponential growth as you follow your heart, there will also be a sense of loss as you let go of the people, places, and things that form the familiarity of your old life. Feeling sadness and loss isn't a sign you made a mistake, did something wrong, or that you're a failure. Sadness is a normal human emotion that comes with loss. Don't try to fix it, push it away, or deny it, all actions that would serve only to take away your energy. Allow yourself to feel your feelings. Cry when you feel like crying.

Keep the Faith

Once you've said yes to your heart, you'll likely find yourself on a new path. There will be ups and downs on the journey. Some things may take a lot longer to materialize than you expected. You may meet with unexpected obstacles, as well as delightful surprises. You may make new companions on the way to your new destination, as well as lose some fellow travelers. You may experience fear as you move toward fulfillment—old fears, new fears, fear of failure, fear you made a mistake, fear you're not doing something right. *Fear is temporary.* However, fulfillment can also be temporary if we base our happiness only on external circumstances or on how our situation appears on the surface.

Fulfillment comes when we leave the doors of our heart open and receptive to our heart's calling and as we support others in following theirs. Keep the faith and don't lose heart.

Trust Your Inner Compass

At times you will meet with rejection, so choose to be unstoppable in your convictions. Stay connected to your innermost being. Let your companions on this courageous journey be faith and an open heart. Keep allowing your heart to open despite life's disappointments, delays, or denials.

And remember, even if you make attempts that fail, no matter how many times, if you are called by your heart and soul to invent something wonderful, new, unique, fascinating, and authentically yours, such as the electric light bulb, like Edison, your success will come as you stay open, playful, curious, and committed. If you trust your inner compass and follow your vision, you'll learn that every ending inevitably births a new beginning, and while you appear to be waiting for something to take hold, a new normal is already emerging..

The choice is yours to make. The journey is about being true to *you*. Connect with your authentic center, allow your natural state of bliss to flourish, and remember, it's never too late to be your self.

Suggestions for *It's Never Too Late to Be Your Self* Study Groups

Here are some suggestions to guide you if you choose to set up a Follow Your Inner Compass and Take Back Your Life Group.

Member Agreements

It can be helpful if members make the following seven agreements to one another:

1. I agree to confidentiality.
2. I agree to speaking from my heart.
3. I agree to show up in a timely manner.
4. I agree to be present in mind, body and spirit.
5. I agree to participate and to be supportive of others in my actions and communications.
6. I agree to read the book and participate in the exercises.

If I am unable to keep any of these agreements, I agree to be transparent about my reasons and seek support from the group members.

Setting Up the Group

Choose a location that is comfortable and private. Agree on whether or not the group will have specific start and ending dates.

Also agree on if the group will be a closed group or an open group.

- Members of closed groups must be present at their first or second meeting and then no new members are added.
- Open groups are where members may join any meeting of the group throughout the duration of the group.

Decide on whether or not this will be a leaderless group or have a regular facilitator. And decide on the number of participants. Ideally, five to ten people.

Decide on the length of each group meeting. Ideally 60–90 minutes.

Course of Study

I recommend devoting one week to a chapter or one week to two chapters if you want a shorter group. Participants should read the chapter(s) in advance and do the invitation(s), then come to group prepared to discuss their experience with the material and the invitation(s).

General Principles for Group Discussion

Agree in advance on the amount of time for personal shares. Remember to hold other group members' shares in confidence and to show one another respect.

Feel free to read significant passages from the book and dive deeper into discussions about the invitations.

Consider using group time for meditation, either beginning or ending the group with meditation.

Create an open, inclusive, and affirming environment and avoid using racist, sexist, or homophobic language. Ask people to share with you their preferred pronouns and use the pronouns they provide (such as she/her, he/his, they/their, ze/zir).

Join the Courageous Heart Community and Enroll in a Webinar or 90-Day Program

Come to my website, DavinaKotulski.com, where you can join my mailing list, register for one of my webinars, or enroll in one of the 90-day Follow Your Inner Compass and Take Back Your Life programs where I will personally guide you through the process of personal transformation.

Acknowledgments

Thank you, Creator, the ultimate artist, from whom all beauty, love, and inspiration flow. I know that I am always divinely guided, guarded, and watched over. I know that I am always loved and encouraged to follow my bliss and supported as I do so. With God, truly all things are possible.

Thank you, Shefali Tsabary, for writing a beautiful foreword. Thank you, Michael Bernard Beckwith, for your powerful introduction. Thank you, Margie Gordillo, for supporting me in answering the call to follow my heart. Thanks to Lisa Felice for connecting me with Margie after I came back from my third trip to Venice and knew I had to quit my job. Gratitude to Reverend Joan Steadman for more than words could express.

Thank you, Mom and Dad, for loving me, supporting me, and telling me I could be whatever I wanted to be. Thank you to my amor, Diana Martin del Campo Leone, for your deep love and support and to my bonus sons, Luca and Dominic, who teach me new ways to be courageous. Thanks to my family of origin, Janice, Rick, Barbara, Chuck, Abs, Richard, Louann, Ray, Amy, Julia, (Rest in peace,

Elaine), Vicki, Chloe, Dylan, Levi, Kathy, Scott, Cutter, and Davis, for just being my beloved family. Gratitude to all the other wonderful people in my life who have been my family in different seasons of my life. Thank you for your blessings.

Special thanks to Jesse Koren, Sharla Jacobs, Robyn Rice-Olmstead, Gil Olmstead, Stephanie Dawn, Natalie Chapron, Megan Walrod, Carol Daly, DJ Sage, and Missy Williker; and to Jessica Colp, who was the catalyst for a huge life change that propelled me to follow my heart to Los Angeles and play a bigger game in a bigger pond. This book would not have been written if we had not met.

Gratitude to the Agape Spiritual Community, especially Anita Rehker, Steven Factor, Karol Mills, Ngozi Ra, Monique Kangarlou, Elizabeth Rice, Juanita Goode, Reverend Kathleen MacNamura, Reverend CoCo Stewart, Charlotte Ciralou, Regina Gibson-Broome, Tunde Illone, Suzi Kessler Lula, and Jami Lula. Thanks to Faleen Campbell, a light to all who knew her. We miss you, yet you've shared from beyond the veil that when we physically die to who we think we are—our bodies and the life we've been living—we open to the truth of who we really are in ways we can't possibly imagine. We step into our infinite selves, pure bodies of light and love.

Thanks to my Los Angeles tribe, especially Jilly Becerra, Karyna Garcia, Audrey Borunda, Karen Lambright, Jenny Karns, Cheryl Leutjen, Eileen Kenny, Charmaine Colina, Shannon Kenny, Philip Eisner, Diane Schroeder, Collin Watts, Adam Burch, Lisa Chan, Stacy Harris, Marianne Emma Jeff and the WBMC Divas, Bianca Peters, Jennifer

Amir, Gerald Wright, Johnny Shaefer, Gayla Turner, Peter Bedard, Jesse Carmichael, and Rick Sudi Karatas.

Gratitude to Tara Zampardi May, Kristen Valus, Becky Robbins, Alice Lancefield, HeatherAsh Amara, Kyle Pivarnik, Laurie York, Carmen Goodyear, Cory Nyamora, Sandy Zeldes, Judith Roberts, Antonia Cruz-Ruiz, Garnet McQuitty, Michael Miller, Shaul Bassi, Martivon Galindo, Terri Fabris, Myra Smith, Mary Durst, Stanley Durst, Renee Baribeau, Stephanie Gunning, Gus Yoo, Sandra Ingerman, Tony Robbins and the Anthony Robbins Foundation, and to the Sounds True team who offered guidance and support and showed me how important it is to be true to your vision and never give up.

Thank you to all the Marriage Equality USA folks who followed their hearts and helped make the world a more equal and just place.

A huge thank you to my clients who trusted me with their dreams and heart's desires and for whom I got to play a supporting role. I am so grateful for each and every one of you who do the work so you can be who really came here to be—YOUR SELF. Shine on!

End Notes

Chapter 1: It's Never Too Late to Be Your Self

Epigraph. Joseph Campbell. *Reflections on the Art of Living: A Joseph Campbell Companion* (New York: HarperCollins Publishers, 1991), p. 15.

1. Center for Behavioral Health Statistics and Quality. "Results from the 2015 National Survey on Drug Use and Health (NSDUH): Detailed Tables," Substance Abuse and Mental Health Services Administration (September 8, 2016), https://www.samhsa.gov/data/sites/default/files/NSDUH-DetTabs-2015/NSDUH-DetTabs-2015/NSDUH-DetTabs-2015.pdf.

2. Anna Robaton. "Why So Many Americans Hate Their Jobs," CBS News/MoneyWatch (March 31, 2017), https://www.cbsnews.com/news/why-so-many-americans-hate-their-jobs.

3. Vincent Manning. "Fond memories of Dom Sebastian Moore, OSB: A personal reflection on the spiritual life," Quest (April 30, 2014), http://questlgbti.uk/fond-memories-of-dom-sebastian-moore-osb-a-personal-reflection-on-the-spiritual-life.

Chapter 2: Open Your Heart

Epigraph. Oprah Winfrey. Found on computer wallpaper.

1. "A Field View of Reality to Explain Human Interconnectedness," HeartMath Institute blog (June 13, 2016), https://www.heartmath.org/articles-of-the-heart/field-view-reality-explain-human-interconnectedness/#more-19123.

2. Rollin McCraty. *The Science of the Heart, Volume 2: Exploring the Role of the Heart in Human Performance* (Boulder Creek, CA.: HeartMath Institute, 2015).

3. Steven M. Morris. "Achieving Collective Coherence: Effects on Heart Rate Variability Coherence and Heart Rhythm Synchronization," *Alternative Therapies in Health and Medicine,* vol 16, no. 4 (July/August 2010), pp. 62–72, https://www.heartmath.org/assets/uploads/2015/01/achieving-collective-coherence.pdf.

4. Rollin McCraty, et al. "The Global Coherence Initiative: Creating a Coherent Planetary Standing Wave," *Global Advances in Health and Medicine,* vol. 1, no. 1 (March 2012), p. 64–77, https://www.ncbi.nlm.nih.gov/pmc/articles/PMC3833489.

Chapter 3: Awaken to Your Authentic Self

Epigraph. William Shakespeare. *Hamlet,* act 1, scene 3.

Chapter 4: Connect with Your Deeper Essence

Epigraph. *Ferris Bueller's Day Off,* written and directed by John Hughes (2006).

1. Thich Nhat Hanh. *You Are Here: Discovering the Magic of the Present Moment* (Boston, MA.: Shambhala Publications, 2009), p. 26.
2. Marie Kondo. *The Life-Changing Magic of Tidying Up: The Japanese Art of Decluttering and Organizing* (Emeryville, CA.: Ten Speed Press, 2014), p. 61.
3. Ibid, p. 42.
4. Denise Mann. "Negative Ions Create Positive Vibes," WebMD (May 6, 2002), https://www.webmd.com/balance/features/negative-ions-create-positive-vibes#1.
5. Paul Grossman, et al. "Mindfulness-based Stress Reduction and Health Benefits A Meta-Analysis," *Journal of Psychosomatic Research,* vol. 57, no. 1 (July 2004): pp. 35–43, https://www.ncbi.nlm.nih.gov/pubmed/15256293.
6. Richard Chambers, et al. "The Impact of Intensive Mindfulness Training on Attentional Control, Cognitive Style, and Affect," *Cognitive Therapy and Research,* vol. 32, no. 3 (June 2008), pp. 303–22, https://link.springer.com/article/10.1007/s10608-007-9119-0.

Chapter 5: Honor Your Intuitive Nudges

Epigraph. Bob Samples. *The Metaphoric Mind: A Celebration of Creative Consciousness.* (Boston, MA.: Addison-Wesley Publishing Company, 1976).

Chapter 6: The Heart of the Matter

Epigraph. Nora Ephron. "Be the Heroine of Your Own Life," Wellesley College Commencement Address, 1996. https://speakola.com/grad/nora-ephron-wellesley-1996

Chapter 7: Take Baby Steps

Epigraph. Martin Luther King, Jr. "The Lost speech and Other Words of Martin Luther King, Jr.," Glossophilia (accessed September 20, 2018), https://www.glossophilia.org/?p=5752.

Chapter 8: Move Through Fear

Epigraph. Anaïs Nin. Goodreads (accessed September 20, 2018), https://www.goodreads.com/quotes/2061-life-shrinks-or-expands-in-proportion-to-one-s-courage.
1. Lisa Nichols. Talk at the Agape International Spiritual Center, May 7, 2017.

Chapter 9: Become Magnetic to Good

Epigraph. William Arthur Ward. Goodreads (accessed September 20, 2018), https://www.goodreads.com/quotes/189187-feeling-gratitude-and-not-expressing-it-is-like-wrapping-a.

1. Oprah Winfrey. *What I Know for Sure* (New York: Flatiron Books 2014), p. 77.
2. Robert A. Emmons and Michael E. McCullough. "Counting Blessings Versus Burdens: An Experimental Investigation of Gratitude and Subjective Wellbeing in Daily Life," *Journal of Personality and Social Psychology, vol. 84, no. 2* (February 2003), pp. 377–89, https://greatergood.berkeley.edu/images/application_uploads/Emmons-CountingBlessings.pdf.
3. Nathaniel M. Lambert and Frank D. Fincham. "Expressing Gratitude to a Partner Leads to More Relationship Maintenance Behavior," *Emotion, vol. 11, no. 1* (February 2011), pp. 52–60, https://www.ncbi.nlm.nih.gov/pubmed/21401225.
4. Merriam-Webster Dictionary online.
5. Roy F. Baumeister, et al. "Bad Is Stronger Than Good," *Review of General Psychology,* vol. 5, no. 4 (2001), pp. 323–70, DOI: 10.1037//1089-2680.5.4.323.
6. Amrisha Vaish, et al. "Not All Emotions Are Created Equal: The Negativity Bias in Social-Emotional Development," *Psychological Bulletin,* vol. 134, no. 3 (May 2008), pp. 383–403, https://www.ncbi.nlm.nih.gov/pubmed/18444702.
7. Ibid.

Chapter 10: Nurture Your Authentic Self

Epigraph. Oscar Wilde. *An Ideal Husband* (Mineola, NY: Dover Publications, 2001).

1. Amy Cuddy. *Presence: Bringing Your Boldest Self to Your Biggest Challenges* (New York: Little, Brown and Company, 2015), p. 51.
2. Ibid.
3. J. David Creswell, et al. (2013). "Self-Affirmation Improves Problem-Solving under Stress," PLOS ONE, vol. 8, no. 5, (May 1, 2013), p. e62593, https://journals.plos.org/plosone/article?id=10.1371/journal.pone.0062593.
4. William Shakespeare. *Hamlet,* act 1, scene 3.

Chapter 11: Embrace Your Wholeness

Epigraph. David Bohm, as cited by Renee Weber. *Dialogues with Scientists and Sages: The Search for Unity* (Routledge & Kegan Paul Books, 1986) by Renée Weber, p. 30, https://archive.org/details/dialogueswithsci00 weberich.

Chapter 12: Let It Go and Move On

Epigraph. Matthew 6: 9–13. The Bible. According to Jon Bloom, "Forgive Us Our What? Three Ways We Say the Lord's Prayer," Desiring God (January 19, 2018), the word *trespasses* first appeared in the Anglican *Book of Common Prayer* in 1549, and as of the 1979 edition it was still being used. See: https://www.desiringgod.org/articles/forgive-us-our-what.

1. Daniel C. Matt. *The Essential Kabbalah: The Heart of Jewish Mysticism* (San Francisco, CA.: HarperSan Francisco, 1995), p. 83.

2. Luke 23: 34. The Bible, King James Version.

3. "Nelson Mandela Transformed Himself and Then His Nation," *Los Angeles Times* (December 2, 2017).

4. Dalai Lama and Howard C. Cutler. *The Art of Happiness: A Handbook for Living* (New York: Riverhead Books, 1998), p. 114.

5. Ibid., p. 259.

6. Edwene Gaines. *The Four Spiritual Laws of Prosperity: A Simple Guide to Unlimited Abundance* (Rodale, 2005), p. 119.

7. Marianne Williamson. *A Return to Love: Reflections on the Principles of 'A Course in Miracles'* (New York: HarperCollins Publishers, 1992), p. 93.

8. Ibid., p. 260.

9. Ibid., p. 101.

10. Colin C. Tipping. *Radical Forgiveness: A Revolutionary Five-Stage Process to Heal Relationships, Let Go of Anger and Blame, and Find Peace in Any Situation* (Boulder, CO.: Sounds True, 2010), p. 287.

11. Ibid., p. 80.

12. Ibid., p. 152.

13. Ibid., p. 297.

Chapter 13: Release Perfectionism

Epigraph. Anne Lamott. *Bird by Bird: Some Instructions on Writing and Life* (New York: Anchor Books, 1994), p. 50.

1. Merriam-Webster Dictionary online.
2. Etienne Benson. "The Many Faces of Perfectionism," *American Psychological Association Monitor*, vol. 34, no. 10 (November 2003), p. 18, http://www.apa.org/monitor/nov03/manyfaces.aspx.
3. Joseph Campbell. *The Hero with a Thousand Faces: Bollingen Series XVII, third edition* (Envato, CA.: New World Library, 2008), p. 298.

Chapter 14: Improve the Quality of Your Relationships

Epigraph. Anthony Robbins. *Unlimited Power* (New York: Free Press, 1986), p. 63.

1. Steven Pressfield. *Turning Pro: Tap Your Inner Power and Create Your Life's Work* (New York: Black Irish Entertainment, 2012), p. 73.
2. Gary Zukav. *Seat of the Soul* (New York: Fireside, 1989), p. 125.
3. Gary Zukav. *Spiritual Partnership: The Journey to Authentic Power* (San Francisco, CA.: HarperOne, 2010), p. xxi.

Chapter 15: Engage the Power of Synergy

Epigraph. Jim Rohn. Goodreads (accessed September 20, 2018), https://www.goodreads.com/quotes/1798-you-are-the-average-of-the-five-people-you-spend.

1. Malcolm Gladwell. *The Tipping Point: How Little Things Can Make a Big Difference* (New York: Little, Brown and Company, 2000), pp. 133–192.
2. "Stanford Prison Experiment," Wikipedia (accessed September 20, 2018), https://en.wikipedia.org/wiki/Stanford_prison_experiment.
3. From a 2001 talk to Dr. Davina Kotulski's Second Chances Program at the Federal Correctional Institution in Dublin, California.
4. Dictionary.com
5. M.T. Hoogwegt, et al. "Exercise Mediates the Association Between Positive Affect and 5-Year Mortality in Patients with Ischemic Heart Disease," *Circulation*, vol. 6, no. 5 (September 1, 2013), pp. 559–66, https://www.ncbi.nlm.nih.gov/pubmed/24021694.
6. Napoleon Hill. *Think and Grow Rich* (1937).
7. Ibid.

Chapter 16: Expect Twists and Turns

Epigraph. Steven Pressfield. *Turning Pro: Tap Your Inner Power and Create Your Life's Work* (New York: Black Irish Entertainment, 2012).

1. Luke 12:32, Holy Bible, King James Version, (with modification of "your Father" to "God").

2. Matthew 13:12, Holy Bible, New International Version, https://biblehub.com/matthew/13-12.htm.
3. Luke 19:26, Holy Bible, New Living Translation, https://biblehub.com/luke/19-26.htm.
4. Shawn Achor. "The Happy Secret to Better Work." TEDx Bloomington (May 2011), https://www.ted.com/talks/shawn_achor_the_happy _secret_to_better_work?language=en.

Chapter 17: Keep the Faith and Follow the Flow

Epigraph. "Is the Universe Friendly?" Awakin (May 7, 2012), http://www.awakin.org/read/view.php?tid=797.
1. Patrick Overton. *The Leaning Tree: [Poems]* (Bloomington, MN.: Bethany Press, 1975).
2. *American Beauty,* screenplay by Alan Ball, directed by Sam Mendes (1999).
3. Woody Allen, as cited by William Safire, *The First Dissident: The Book of Job in Today's Politics* (New York: Random House, 1992).
4. "Katy Perry," Wikipedia (accessedSeptember 21, 2018), https://en.wikipedia.org/wiki/Katy_Perry. Also *Katy Perry: Part of Me,* directed by Dan Cutforth and Jane Lipsitz (2012).

Chapter 18: Expect and Respect Your Metamorphosis

Epigraph. Christiane Northrup. *The Wisdom of Menopause: Creating Physical and Emotional Health during Menopause,* revised edition (New York: Bantam Books, 2012), p.78.
1. William Bridges. *Transitions: Making Sense of Life's Changes* (Boston, MA.: Addison-Wesley, 1980).
2. Ibid., pp. 119–20.
3. Ibid., p. 121.
4. Michael Bernard Beckwith. *Life Visioning: A Transformative Process for Activating Your Unique Gifts and Highest Potential* (Boulder, CO.: Sounds True, 2012), p. 88.
5. Originally published in 1875. Mary Baker Eddy. *Science and Health with Key to the Scriptures* (Boston, MA.: Christian Science Publishing Society), p. 401, https://www.christianscience.com/the-christian-science-pastor/science-and-health.
6. Barbara M. Vining. "What Is Chemicalization?" *Christian Science Journal* (February 1994), https://journal.christian-science.com/shared/view/1u61ntaeisk.
7. Eddy.
8. Ibid.

Chapter 19: Turning Your Heart's Desires into Gold

Epigraph. Walt Disney. Goodreads (accessed September 20, 2018), https://www.goodreads.com/quotes/3244957-all-of-our-dreams-can-come-true-if-we-have.

1. Carl G. Jung. *Psychology and Alchemy: Collected Works, Volume 12* (London, U.K.: Routledge, 1968). Jung also writes about alchemy in his 1964 book *Memories, Dreams, and Reflections* (reissue: New York: Vintage Books, 1989), p. 209.
2. Paulo Coelho. *The Alchemist* (New York: HarperCollins Publishers, 1993), p. 150.
3. Matthew Human website: http://www.matthewhuman.com.
4. *Occupy Love*, written and directed by Velcrow Ripper (2013), http://occupylove.org.
5. You can read more about the history of Edgefield and learn about these alchemists at http://www.mcmenamins.com/1171-history-of-edgefield.

Chapter 20: Don't Get Bitter, Make It Better

Epigraph. John Wooden, as cited by Craig Impelman. "Make Each Day Your Masterpiece," Success Presents: Coach John Wooden (January 18, 2017), https://www.the-woodeneffect.com/your-masterpiece.

1. Marcos Apolonio, as cited by Davina Kotulski. *How to Come Out of the Closet and Into Your Power* (2011).

2. Norma Hotaling, as cited in 2012 on now-defunct Standing Against Global Exploitation Website. To find SAGE San Francisco, visit the organization's Facebook page: https://www.facebook.com/The-SAGE-Project-Inc-274734426601.

Chapter 21: Set Boundaries

Epigraph. Melody Beattie. *Codependent No More: How to Stop Controlling Others and Start Caring for Yourself* (Center City, MN.: Hazelden Publishing, 1986), p. 116.

1. Ibid., 84.
2. Ibid., p. 36.

Chapter 22: Own Your Life

Epigraph. Steve Jobs. "'You've got to find what you love,' Jobs says," Stanford News (June 14, 2005), https://news.stanford.edu/2005/06/14/jobs-061505.

Resources

Now that you've begun your journey to follow your heart and take back your life, you'll continue to grow in courage and authentic self-expression every day if you keep putting the tools and strategies in this book to work for you. To help you stay on this path without faltering and go deeper than you can with a book alone, I created the following additional resources for you.

Visit My Websites

To inquire about having me speak to your group or to work with me one on one as your coach, visit DavinaKotulski.com. I am available for therapy in person or via video conferencing in California State only. I am available for one-on-one coaching in person in the Los Angeles area and via telephone or video conference everywhere else.

Come to FollowYourCourageousHeart.com to get your free downloadable worksheets, "How to Hearticulate™ Your Desires" and "It's Never Too Late Self-Care Assessment," as well as to register for a free "Be Your Own

Hero" webinar and the "Follow Your Courageous Heart" home study program.

Join Me on the Social Networks

Facebook.com/DrDavinaKotulski

Twitter.com/DrKotulski

Instagram.com/DrKotulski

linkedin.com/in/DrDavinaKotulski

Courageous Heart Community Facebook Group

https://www.facebook.com/groups/courageousheart

ABOUT THE AUTHOR

Davina Kotulski, Ph. D., is a licensed clinical psychologist, sought-after speaker, and author with a thriving private therapy practice in Los Angeles, California, and an international life coaching practice. She facilitates workshops and webinars on following your courageous heart, past-life regression, mysticism, spiritual growth, self-empowerment, and authentic self-expression.

After receiving her doctorate in clinical psychology in 1996, Davina worked for over thirteen years as a psychologist in a federal prison, leading empowerment workshops with female inmates, introducing them to the teachings of self-empowerment authors, such as Thich Nhat Hahn, Napoleon Hill, and Tony Robbins.

Davina was the executive director of Marriage Equality USA. She has received notable awards for her civil rights advocacy, including the Saints Alive Award from the Metropolitan Community Church, the Michael Switzer Leadership Award, and Grand Marshal, San Francisco LGBT Pride Parade. As a respected leader in the LGBT equality movement, Davina Kotulski has appeared in dozens of documentary films, been a guest on television (notably on CNN) and on National Public Radio and the talk shows of numerous other radio stations, and has been featured in print publications, like *Newsweek, USA Today, San Francisco Chronicle, L.A. Times, Oregonian,* to name a few. She was a guest therapist on the show *Please Understand Me* produced by Sarah Silverman.

Davina's previous books include *Why You Should Give a Damn about Gay Marriage, Love Warriors: The Rise of the Marriage Equality Movement and Why It Will Prevail,* and the novel *Behind Barbed Eyes.* Her written work has been featured in periodicals, anthologies, online magazines, and blogs.

Dr. Davina Kotulski lives in Los Angeles, California.

About Red Ink Press

The mission of Red Ink Press is to uplift our readers with inspirational and entertaining fiction and nonfiction that empowers readers to move beyond fear and perceived limitations to be their best and highest selves and create a world where love prevails.

Red Ink Press was founded in 2016 to give voice to authors, characters and topics that are underrepresented in mainstream media.

Red Ink Press publishes inspirational fiction and nonfiction with a focus on personal growth, self-empowerment, spirituality, and mind-body-spirit. Red Ink Press is committed to supporting authors who have a powerful message to share with stories of transformation, inspiration and redemption.

We also provide inspirational online courses and in-person events.